ناصر رباح

GAZA: THE POEM SAID ITS PIECE

NASSER RABAH

TRANSLATED FROM THE ARABIC BY
AMMIEL ALCALAY, EMNA ZGHAL,
AND KHALED AL-HILLI

CITY LIGHTS BOOKS
SAN FRANCISCO

Front cover photograph of the author by Mosab Abu Toha,
taken in Gaza City on January 9, 2022.
Cover design by Megan Jones
Interior design by Victor Mingovits
Arabic calligraphy by Khaled al-Hilli

Library of Congress Cataloging-in-Publication Data

Names: Rabah, Nasser author. | Alcalay, Ammiel, translator. | Zghal, Emna, translator. | Al-Hilli, Khaled, translator. | Rabah, Nasser. Gaza. | Rabah, Nasser. Gaza. Arabic.
Title: Gaza : the poem said its piece / Nasser Rabah ; translated from Arabic by Ammiel Alcalay, Emna Zghal, Khaled al-Hilli.
Description: San Francisco, CA : City Lights Books, 2025. | Series: Pocket poets ; 64 | Parallel text in Arabic and English. |
Identifiers: LCCN 2024047584 | ISBN 9780872869127 (paperback)
Subjects: LCSH: Rabah, Nasser--Translations into English. | LCGFT: Poetry.
Classification: LCC PJ7960.A16 G3913 2025 | DDC 892.7/17--dc23/eng/20241029
LC record available at https://lccn.loc.gov/2024047584

City Lights Books are published at the
City Lights Bookstore, 261 Columbus Avenue,
San Francisco, CA 94133.
www.citylights.com

The following poems in translation have previously appeared in these journals and online magazines:

"A House That Looks Like Your Laugh" *O Bod*
"Background Music for Life" and "In the Endless War"
Michigan Quarterly Review
"Dead Cats Continue to Meow" *LitHub*
"Untitled" *New Yorker*
"Statues of Flesh and Blood" *Words Without Borders*
"Gaza . . . Gaza" *Harper's Magazine*

فهرس

مفتتح 2
ماء عطش لماء 4
باب النص 6
غزة . . غزة 8
شرفة معلقة في السماء 10
لا بريد منذ سنوات 14
كنت تراباً 16
خارجا إلى ذهولي 18
عكاز الأعمى 22
نبي الضلال 24
الشجرة التي لم يفهمها أحد 26
شجيرة الحجارة 28
ملائكة قدامى 30
أرواح ليلية 32
أحلام مشوّهة 34
ملائكة صغار 36
بيت يشبه ضحكتك 38
غياب مبكر 44
كعكة على شكل قلب 46
مديح الهواء 50
معراج 52
مقاطع قصيرة 54

TABLE OF CONTENTS

Prelude 3
Water Thirsty for Water 5
The Gate of Text 7
Gaza . . . Gaza 9
A Balcony Hanging in the Sky 11
No Mail for Years 15
I Was Sand 17
Getting Out to My Stupor 19
The Blind Man's Cane 23
Prophet of the Lost Way 25
The Tree Nobody Understood 27
Stone Sapling 29
Angels of Old 31
Nocturnal Spirits 33
Distorted Dreams 35
Little Angels 37
A House That Looks Like Your Laugh 39
Early Absence 45
Heart-Shaped Cake 47
The Flattery of Air 51
Ascension 53
Small Fragments 55

تأملات 62
أثر فراشتك 78
مكنسة الخراب 80
أطهو أنيني 82
حديقة الجنون 84
سطوع العاديّة 86
ما لم أقله لي 90
موسيقى خلفية للحياة 128
قطط ميتة تواصل المواء 138
على من نقرأ الوقت 140
في الحرب التي لا تنتهي 142
قالت القصيدة كلمتها 148
تماثيلَ من لحمٍ ودمٍ 152
بدون عنوان 154
خارج من البيت 156
آخر الجنود 158
غضب 160
جوع 162
فتات الكراسي 164
ساحة من رماد 166

Meditations 63
The Trace of Your Butterfly 79
Havoc's Broom 81
Stewing My Groans 83
The Garden of Madness 85
Radiance of the Ordinary 87
What I Didn't Say to Me 91
Background Music for Life 129
Dead Cats Continue to Meow 139
To Whom Should We Recite the Time 141
In the Endless War 143
The Poem Said Its Piece 149
Statues of Flesh and Blood 153
Untitled 155
Leaving the House 157
The Last of the Soldiers 159
Rage 161
Hunger 163
Pieces of Chairs 165
Plaza of Ash 167

FOREWORD

In 2020, I had the idea of starting a literary magazine featuring writers from the Gaza Strip with the goal of introducing their work to the outside world. I shared my vision with many friends in the United States and England, who all thought it was an important project to support, and a few contributed financially. One friend, Ammiel Alcalay spread the word among his circle and asked if he could help translate poems for the not-yet-born magazine. I assembled the works of six excellent writers to share with Ammiel, including the poetry of Nasser Rabah.

I first met Nasser when he reached out to me in the summer of 2017 through my younger brother, Hamza, a scholar of Arabic grammar and literature. Nasser would sometimes consult with Hamza about inflections on some words and whether the structure of a certain sentence was still an Arabic one. I don't remember a time when I met with Nasser or spoke with him on the phone when he did not ask if I could help translate and submit his poems to American publications. I always sensed how frustrating it was for him not to see his poems shared with others around the world. As a Palestinian writer, I know how suffocating it feels to remain stuck in Gaza, you and your writing.

If I were to pick only one poet from Gaza to be translated and published in the English-speaking world, this is who it would be. Nasser Rabah is my favorite living poet in Palestine. The language he uses in his poems is dazzling. His metaphors are like raindrops pouring over me after a long summer. The musicality of his lines could replace my heartbeats and I would feel more than alive.

While Nasser's personal library now lies buried under the rubble of his house in the al-Maghazi Camp in the middle of the Gaza Strip, the poems have survived and are now destined to be read by thousands of readers, both in Arabic and English, here in the pages of Nasser's first book in translation. This revelatory collection gathers poems from three of his five published poetry books, and includes new work written during the ongoing onslaught against Palestine and Palestinian life in its every aspect.

The "poem said its piece," and the responsibility now lies with us, readers and witnesses, to confront the implications for ourselves.

Mosab Abu Toha
Displaced from Gaza

إلى روح أبي
معلمي الأول.
إلى روح أمي
حبي الذي لا يموت.

To the spirit
of my Father
my first teacher.
To the spirit
of my Mother
my undying love.

غزة

قالت القصيدة كلمتها

GAZA: THE POEM SAID ITS PIECE

مُفتَتح

يا ربّ..

هَذي روحي، نضجَتْ في أبجديّةِ اللّه حينَ قلتَ لي: كُنْ، فكانتْ تسيلُ منها القصيدةُ، تهرولُ باتجاهِ اكتمالٍ، وحيثُ الكمالُ انتهاءٌ. أينما رميتُ عَصاي فاضتْ ثعابينُ روحي، واهتزّتْ شفةُ الشوقِ لحليبِ امرأةٍ من غمامٍ. كانَ الجسدُ المنسيُّ على نارِ اللغةِ يفيضُ ذهولاً ومزاميرَ، وطوالَ الوقتِ أُمرِّرُ مِن ثقبِ إبرتِه جِمالَ رُؤاي. اثنينِ كنّا ملِكٌ ومملكةٌ مِن كتابةٍ. فيا ربّ هي ذِي رُوحي ملّث كلاماً، وصارتْ جاهزةً للقِطافِ.

PRELUDE

O Lord . . .
This my soul, ripened in God's alphabet when you said to me:
Be — then the poem flowed, hastening to its completion, where
perfection is an end. Wherever I cast my staff, the serpents of
my soul overflow and a yearning lip quivers for the milk of a
woman made of clouds. The body forgotten on language's fire
brims over as astonishments and psalms, and I pass, all the
time, through the eye of its needle, the camels of my visions.
We were two, a king and a kingdom of writing, O Lord,
here's my soul, done with words, now ripe for the picking.

ماءٌ عَطِشٌ لماء

يحدثُ أنْ ألُمَّ فراغاً عَميقاً بجَيبِ القميصِ، أركضُ كأنَّ لديَّ مَشاغلَ أو أنَّ وهما ما يلاحقني، وقدْ يبادلُني الفراغُ التَّحِيَّةَ؛ لنَفتَرِقَ عندَ ناصيةِ قصيدةٍ جديدةٍ، أتركُهُ يُفَتِّشُ عن مقاعدَ فارغةٍ في قلوبٍ حزينةٍ، عن سربِ أنّاتٍ تسيلُ من ناي يكسرُ الآنَ صيامَه. يُباركُ نصفَ صحونِنا العِجافِ بنصفِها المُعافِ. فراغي شيخٌ مطرودٌ من رحمةِ فُقَراء وأزقّةٍ، ينحتونَ الوقتَ مِن أجلِ شربةِ ماءٍ، وأنا أنحتُ من اللغةِ سرابي وأُباهي. أيّها الوغدُ المسنُّ، تعالَ جالِسْني فلا شيءَ نفعلُهُ، تعالَ فنحنُ مُتشابهانِ إلى حدِّ المللِ.

WATER THIRSTY FOR WATER

It just so happens that I gather emptiness in my shirt pocket
and run like I have things to do or I'm chased by some
illusion, emptiness might exchange greetings with me and then we
part ways at the first line of a new poem, I leave it searching
for vacant seats in sad hearts, for a flock of woe flowing from
a flute just breaking its fast. It blesses the meager half of our
plate with its fulsome half. My emptiness is an old man expelled
from the mercy of the poor and of the alleys, sculpting time
for a drink of water, and I sculpt my mirage out of language
and brag. Come, sit with me, you old rascal, there's nothing
doing, we're so annoyingly alike, to the point of utter tedium.

بابُ النَّصِ

ليتَ هذا البابُ لي فأكسره،
وأمضي مثل غيمةٍ بلا طريق.
لكنه بابٌ مراوغٌ يرتدي أخشابَهُ حين أفقدُ المفتاح،
ويصبحُ بركةَ ماءٍ لو معي مفتاحه!
وأحملُ نحوَهُ دلوَ الماء فيرجع الباب باباً خشبياً.
في حلمي يصيرُ نافذةً وأصحو يصيرُ سوراً وجدار،
أي تجربة هذه يا رب؟
وهذا أي باب؟
وهذا الضجيج الذي يملأُ الآن وقتي حيلةٌ أخرى؟
أم هي المخيلةُ مشرعةً على الفراغ؟

THE GATE OF TEXT

If only this gate was mine, I'd break it,
and pass through like a cloud with no trail.
But it's a tricky gate, donning its timbers when I lose the key,
and turning into a puddle of water when I have it!
I go at the gate with a bucket of water,
and it turns back into a wooden gate.
In my dream, it becomes a window and I wake up
and it turns into a wall.
What kind of business is this, O Lord?
And what gate?
And is all this racket now taking up my time another ruse?
Or is it imagination opening wide onto the void?

غزة . . . غزة

الهدايا التي لم أرسلها إليكِ في عيدِ ميلادِ الحرب،
تلويحةُ القصيدةِ لي وأنا أغلقُ كتابي؛ كأنها تموتُ بالغرغرينا،
الجسورُ المغلقةُ بين فمي وكلامي عن كلِّ شيء،
التكناتُ المحاذيةُ لسياجِ حياتي العالي،
مشاويرُ جيراني القدامى قبلَ أن يتناثروا مع قذيفةِ الغياب،
أحلامي التي تمشي مع عكازِها الهرمِ نحو بحرٍ لا يهتمُ بهما،
حبةُ الدواءِ الأخيرة في خِزانةِ الأمل،
حباتُ مسبحتي التي لا تنتهي، وأنا أهذي: غزة .. غزة.
مثلُ أعلامِ بلادٍ هَزَمت نفسها،
من القلبِ إلى القلبِ عادوا ساهمين،
يفتشون عن العناوين القديمةِ في بريد مالحٍ.
عن أغنياتٍ طرّزوها على ثوبِ الرمال،
فيسيلُ القلبُ نهراً من ندمٍ مصفّى،
يدورُ كزهرة العبّادِ مثل اسمِ ميتٍ لحبيبة، ويخترع الحمام.
عادوا إلى القلب عادوا، عراةً من حنينهم،
مرتبكين كيف سيفتحون حقيبة الغياب فتنهمرُ الأفاعي،
وأنا أهذي: غزة . . . غزة.

GAZA . . . GAZA

The gifts I didn't send you on war's birthday, the poem's
wave to me as I close the book, like it was dying of gangrene,
the bridges between my mouth and what I would say about
anything shut down, the barracks next to the tall fence of
my life, the time spent with old neighbors before they
were scattered by the shell of absence, my dreams
walking along with their old cane to a sea that
couldn't care less, last pill in the cabinet
of hope, the beads in my rosary are
endless, and I'm delirious: Gaza . . . Gaza.
Like flags of a country that defeated itself,
from the heart to the heart they came back staring
into the void, looking for old addresses in the salty mail.
As for the songs embroidered on the dress of sand,
the heart flows like a river of purified regret,
whirling like a sunflower, like a name
dead to the lover, inventing doves.
Back to the heart, they came back, stripped of their longing,
nervous about how to open the suitcase of absence
and let the snakes pour out, I am delirious: Gaza . . . Gaza.

شرفةٌ معلّقةٌ في السماءِ

لستُ جندياً ولكنّي رأيتُني في الحربِ بِسُترةٍ عسكريّةٍ حينَ أشتري الخبزَ، وحينَ أنامُ، وحينَ أُبعَثُ بَعْدَ آخِرِ الأخبارِ حيّاً. أُنسِّقُ البارودَ على جانبَي طريقِ المقبرةِ، أزرعُ ما تيسَّرَ من شظايا في حقولِ الذاكرةِ كلّما يحصدُ النسيانُ مغفرةً وأصدقاءَ، كلما قطعوا ذراعِيَ أرفعُ رايةَ السأمِ التي لا تنحني. أُوصِلُ الأبناءَ للآباءِ، والفقراءَ للفقراءِ، أكملُ عدَّ دمعِ الأمهاتِ لمسبحةِ الحكايةِ.

أنيرُ عتمةَ القلبِ بشمعِ الخوفِ، أوزّعُهُ على الحيطانِ — عندما يبدأُ القصفُ — آيةً آيةً. أرمِّمُ ما تهدمَ من جدارِ الوقتِ، أقطِفُ ما تفتَّحَ مِنْ رصاصِ أعدائي، أعلِّمُ الأولادَ — إنْ كَبروا – مواقيتَ الصلاةِ على البلادِ.

لستُ جندياً ولكنّي رأيتُني في الحربِ شُرفةً مُعلَّقةً في السماءِ بعدما اغتالوا البنايةَ، أرقبُ كيفَ يهرعُ الجيرانُ نحوَ شواطئِ الأسفلتِ قبلَ موجةِ القصفِ الجديدةِ، كيفَ تنجو من اصابتِها البيوتُ بِفعلِ أخطاءِ طيّارٍ حديثِ السنِّ، وبراعةِ صاحبِ الكاميرا الذي حملَ صورتَها إلى المَشفَى، وصدفةَ أنْ وجَدوا طبيباً ماهراً في إصاباتِ البيوتِ، وكيفَ سيارةُ الإسعافِ تجلسُ عندَ بابِ القهرِ مثلَ امرأةٍ ذوّبَها الحملُ، ودوّخَتْها شمسُ آب.

لستُ جندياً ولكني رأيتُني في الحربِ ملائكةً أصفّقُ للجنودِ، أمّاً تغسلُ الأكفانَ، بيتاً يشدُّ ثيابَ سُكّانٍ، عادوا كلّما خَرجوا كي يطمئنَّ البيتُ، أدلُّ — رأيتُني — على جيبي بريدَ القذيفةِ، ثمَّ أجعِّدُها مِثلَ فاتورةِ كهرباءَ أحفظُ للأولادِ طابَتهم لِبَعْدِ الحربِ، ربّما عادوا بلا سيقانٍ، أنتظرُ البكاءَ فلا يجيءُ لأنّه مِثلي أضاعَ في الحربِ ساعتَهُ وظِلَّهُ، وظَلَّ هكذا بلا

A BALCONY HANGING IN THE SKY

I am no soldier, but I see myself in uniform during the war
when buying bread, when sleeping, and when I get resurrected
after the latest news. I arrange gunpowder on both sides
of the road leading to the cemetery, I plant whatever
shrapnel comes in handy in the fields of memory anytime
forgetfulness reaps forgiveness and friends, each time they
sever my arm, I raise the flag of tedium that never bends,
I bring together children and parents, the poor and the poor,
and I finish counting mothers' tears for the prayer beads
of the story. I light the darkness of the heart with the candle
of fear, I dole it out on the walls — when the bombing starts —
a verse, a verse each. I restore what has been demolished of
the walls of time, I pick what has blossomed of my enemy's
ammunition, and I teach the kids — if they ever grow older —
the timetable to pray for the country. I am no soldier, but
during the war I see myself a balcony hanging in the sky
after they kill the building, I watch how the neighbors rush
to asphalt beaches before the new wave of bombing,
how homes survive their injuries because of a novice pilot's
error, the talent of a cameraman who brought their picture
to the hospital, and the luck they had in finding a doctor
skilled in home injuries, and how the ambulance stands
by at the gate of injustice, like a woman pregnancy
exhausted and the August sun made faint.
I am no soldier, but I see myself during the war an angel

أصدقاءَ.
مَنْ يرفعُ الأولادَ نحو اللّهِ قبل صليبِهم؟ مَنْ يوقفُ الأحياءَ من الطوافِ حولَ نشرةِ الأخبارِ؟ مِنَ الجُرفِ المُطِلِّ على الخُرافةِ؟ مَنْ يُعطي المدينةَ حقّها في الخبزِ قبلَ النومِ والميناءِ؟ أنْ تمشي على مَهَلٍ كأيٍّ مدينةٍ على ماءِ الحياةِ؟
مَنْ يُخرج المدنيَّ مِنْ سُترةِ الجنديِّ، والجنديَّ مِنْ سُترةِ السياسيِّ، والسياسيَّ من سُترةِ الدينيِّ، والدينيَّ من سُترةِ الحمقى؟ مَنْ يُخْرِجُ المدينةَ مِنْ تَنَكُّرِ الثيابِ للثيابِ؟
لستُ جندياً ولكنّي رأيتُني في الحربِ أرتّبُ مشهدَ الموتِ الأخيرَ؛ حتّى يُعجبَ الأحياءَ مَوتي.

applauding soldiers, a mother washing shrouds, a home
reassured by hanging on to the clothes of residents who
return every time they leave. I see myself, I guide the missile
mail to my pocket, then I crumble it like an electric bill.
I save their ball for the kids for after the war. They might
return with no legs. I wait for the tears, but they don't
come — they too, like me, lost their watch and shadow
during the war and remained like that with no friends.
Who will raise the children to God before their cross?
Who will stop the living from circling around the news
like pilgrims? Who from the cliff overlooking the myth?
Who will give the city its share of bread before sleep
and a harbor for it to walk slowly like any other
city on the water of life?
Who will pull the civilian out of the military uniform,
the military from the uniform of the politician,
the politician from the uniform of the clergy,
and the clergy from the uniform of fools.
And who will pull the city out from
clothes double-crossing clothes?
I'm no soldier, but I see myself during the war arranging the
scene of the last death, to please with my death the living.

لا بريد منذ سنوات

لا بريدَ منذُ سنواتٍ، كلُّ ما أجدُه في يدي كلَّ صباحٍ مُجرّدُ كلماتٍ غامضةٍ مُبعثرَةٍ، أبدّدُ اليومَ كلَّه في إعادةِ ترتيبِها دونَ جدوَى، كلماتٌ مِثلَ حُلْمٍ لا يُفسَّرُ، لغةٌ ليستْ لي محفورةٌ على حجرِ الوقتِ البارِدِ، ضوضاءُ هائلةٌ في سوقٍ شعبيٍّ حيثُ أنا بضاعةٌ كاسدةٌ، لا جملةَ واحدةً مفيدةً، لا سطرَ يبلّلُ الشوقَ لخبرٍ مُؤكَّدٍ، لا شيءَ يمنحُكَ فرحاً كاملاً أو حُزناً كاملاً. لا بريدَ منذُ سنواتٍ، فمَن سيراسلُ شخصاً ميّتاً!

NO MAIL FOR YEARS

No mail for years, all I find in my hand every morning
is merely obscure scattered words, I waste the whole day
rearranging them in vain, a word like a dream that can't
be interpreted, a language not mine engraved on the cold
stone of time, the racket and din of a street market where
I'm leftover goods. Not one full sentence or line whets
the desire for news I can verify, nothing to impart
real joy or sadness. No mail for years —
who'd want to write to a dead man?

كنت تراباً

كنت تراباً يتخللُني العشبُ كدغدغةٍ خفيفةٍ، تَعبرُني الغيومُ أو الفتياتُ حين يخرجن من بابِ مدرسةٍ قريبةٍ، يغسلُني المطرُ والبَرَدُ وتلوحُني الشمسُ والمحاريثُ في مرورِها الباهتِ على حقلِ حنطةٍ في النواحي البعيدةِ لقريةٍ باهتةٍ. كنتُ تراباً كأي ترابٍ منذوراً لبساطتهِ لا يشغلُه الوقتُ، ولا تهمُه المسافةُ والعابرون. في ظَهيرةٍ لم أعذ أذكرُ إلا ظهيرتَها الناتئةَ كمسمارٍ في حائطٍ، لم أرهُم حين جلبوا الماءَ وجَبَلوا ترابي فأُغشي علي. لم أدركْ حقيقةَ أمري إلا بعدَ سنواتٍ من إفاقتي المرعبةِ أحدقُ في مشهدٍ واحدٍ مكرور، عندما أدركتُ أنني أصبحت حجراً في زنزانةٍ! حجرٌ يحدقُ في جدارٍ أعمى طوالَ الوقتِ، يعدُ أيامَهُ بجروحٍ يحزُها السجناءُ على صمتِهِ البارد، بالموتى المغادرينَ، بالآتينَ إليّ حاملينَ على ظهورِهِم المنكسرةِ حقيبةَ الأملِ. الأملُ الذي تركتُه هناك مبعثراً في ظهيرةِ حقلٍ بعيدٍ بعيدْ.

I WAS SAND

I was sand gently grazed by grass woven through me.
Clouds pass me over, or girls as they come out the gate
of a nearby school. Rain and hail wash me, and the sun
and plows bear down on me in their dull movement over
a wheat field in the far-flung reaches of a nondescript village.
I was sand, like any other, so ordained for my simplicity
that time was of no concern to me, nor distance, nor the
passersby. One afternoon — I only remember it now sticking
its back out like a nail on a wall — I didn't see them when they
brought the water to mix with my sand and I fainted. I only found
out the truth about myself years after my horrific awakening,
staring at a single scene, repeating over and over.
I realized that I'd become a stone in a prison cell.
A stone staring at a blind man's wall hours on end, counting
its days by the wounds prisoners etched on its cold silence,
by the departing dead, by those coming in carrying on their
broken backs a suitcase of hope. Hope I left behind,
scattered on an afternoon of a far, far-flung field.

خارجاً إلى ذهولي

١

خارجا إلى ذهولي، قالَ السجنُ: خذْ رائحتي معكَ.
قلتُ: سأخلعُ عندَ البابِ ثيابي، قال السجنُ: رائحتي صداً يتسلقُ الذكرياتِ، ستخرجُ مني، فأسجنُ فيكَ. نظلُ معاً حتى تنفرطَ ذاكرتُكَ كمسبحةٍ، فينتهي حينها عذابُكَ، تضحكُ دونما سعادةٍ، تبكِي دونما ألمٍ، تحدقُ في فراغِكَ الأبديِّ.
قال السجنُ: أنا صمتُكَ المكترثُ بأسئلةِ المسافةِ والمدى، أنا روحُكَ التي سكبْتَها لدي، ملامحُكَ التي شيئاً فشيئاً تأخذُ شكلَ غرفةٍ صغيرةٍ فارغة.

٢

لم يكسر السجنُ روحه،
فتح غطاءَ عطرها فقط.
الروحُ تبخرت في الباحةِ المسيَّجة،
وتعطنت الثمالةُ في ظلمةِ الانتظار.

GETTING OUT TO MY STUPOR

1

Getting out to my stupor, the prison said: take my scent
with you. I said: I'll take my clothes off at the door.
Prison said: My scent is rust that climbs memories,
you'll get out of me and I'll stay caged in you.
We'll be together until your memory breaks like prayer beads,
then your torment will end. You'll laugh without joy,
cry without pain, and stare into your perpetual void.
Prison said: I'm your silence, my concerns
are matters of distance and scale.
I'm the soul you once poured into me, bit by bit
your features will look like a small, empty room.

2

Prison didn't break his spirit,
it just took the lid off its perfume,
the soul evaporated in the fenced-in yard,
and the dregs putrefied in the darkness of waiting.

٣

على جدران السجن تركنا خلفنا أظافرنا،
تنمو في الظلمة كعلّيقَةٍ ملعونة.
يتجلى عليها الحقد . . . كلما نسينا.

٤

فاراً من زرقة سجنه، قفز الأزرق من لوحته نحو البحر.

٥

الزهور لا تنمو في السجن . . . الهواء مالح، والتربة دم.

٦

عاد السجين إلى بيته . . . فلم يجده،
عاد إلى عمره . . . فلم يجده،
لم يجد غير حيرته سلماً، صعد منه إلى قلبي.

3

We left our fingernails on the prison walls,
growing in the dark like a cursed vine.
Baring its malice . . . every time we forget.

4

Fleeing the blueness of its prison, blue jumped from
the painting to the sea.

5

Flowers don't grow in prison . . . the air is salty,
and the soil blood.

6

The prisoner goes back home . . . and can't find it,
goes back to his life . . . and can't find it.
with bewilderment his only ladder, he reached my heart.

عكاز الأعمى

تماماً مثل ملمسِ حلم نسيته حين صحوت،
كطعمِ شرفةٍ لا يُطلُّ منها أحد،
وأنا أشرب شارعاً وأمشي،
أرتكزُ على مقولاتٍ خاطئة وأواصلُ البعاد؛
أعمى بعكازٍ من ذكريات عمياء.
من يُعيدُ لي قطيعَ الحنين لأذبحه واحداً واحداً بالغناء؟
من يُصفّرُ لي عند أرجوحة ندمي فأصحو،
وأسكبُ وقتي جِوارَ الوسادةِ وأنساه مثل حلمٍ خشن،
أو شارعٍ بطعمِ المتاهة؟
كل رماد يفسر الغابة،
وكل قصيدة تفسر الهباء.

THE BLIND MAN'S CANE

Just like the texture of a dream I forget upon waking,
like the taste of a balcony nobody looks out from,
I drink a street and go,
I lean on false statements and stray further,
a blind man with a cane made of blind memories.
Who can bring me back the herd of yearning to slaughter it
one by one with song?
Who whistles to me by the swing of my regret so I wake up
and spill my time by the pillow to forget it like a coarse dream,
or a street tasting of labyrinth?
Every ash spells forest,
and every poem spells scattered dust.

نبيُّ الضلال

أنا النبيُ الذي فقدَ نبوءَتَهُ، وضعتُ كتابي على الرصيفِ، وجلستُ عليهِ. كلَ يومٍ أنزهُ نهرَ الضلالِ في شوارعِ البلدةِ، وحينَ أعودُ إلى البيتِ أعلقُهُ على حائطِ اليقينِ، فأحلمُ ببلادٍ ميْتَةٍ لها رائحةُ حقيبةٍ قديمةٍ، بنساءٍ حجرياتٍ يرمينَ نهودَهُنَ عليّ كأحذيةٍ، بزهورٍ سوداءَ تخرجُ من نايي لتضيءَ كوابيسي بالأرقِ. مث قليلاً أيها الكلامُ لأنامَ وأحلمَ بأناسٍ بكمٍ، يمشون كشجرٍ ويهتفونَ كريحٍ. مث قليلاً أيها الكلامُ كي أبدلَ قصائدي الرثةَ بنظراتٍ ساهمةٍ وغيومٍ خفيفة، وأرشقها كريشةٍ في قلبي. مث قليلاً، وهاتِ قُبلَتي الأولى؛ نجمةً أتوكأُ عليها وأهشُ بها على ألمي. أريدُ النبيَ الذي كُنتُهُ، أريدُ النبيَ الذي خُنتُهُ.

PROPHET OF THE LOST WAY

I am the prophet who lost his prophecy. I put my book
on the sidewalk and sat on it. Everyday I dry the River of
Misdirection along the streets of town, and when I get back
home, I hang it on the Wall of Certainty and dream of a dead
country that smells of an old suitcase, of women made of
stone who hurl their breasts at me like shoes, and of black
flowers that come out of my flute to light up my nightmares
with sleeplessness. Die a little, O Speech, so I can sleep and
dream of the mute, walking like trees and chanting like wind.
Die a little, O Speech, so I can trade my tattered poems for
vacant stares and light clouds to cast them like a feather
into my heart. Die a little, and give me my first kiss: a star
to lean on and herd my pain with. I want the prophet
that I was. I want the prophet I betrayed.

الشجرةُ التي لمْ يفهمْها أحدٌ

كتابةٌ أولى

لم يكنْ ليدركَ البستانيُّ العجوزُ وهو ينسى معطفَه على غُصنِ شجرةٍ نائيةٍ بغابةٍ حزينةٍ أنّه يثيرُ حيرتَها الأبديةَ وحاجَتها المريرةَ في حياكةِ دهشةِ العابرين، أنْ تكونَ شجرةً نادرةً تزهرُ معاطفَ وأرديةً ملوّنةً وشالاتِ حريرٍ يقطفُها المُحبّونَ في مرورِهم الناعسِ تحتَ ظلالِها الناعسةِ.
نجّارٌ نَزِقٌ عبَرَ الغابةَ متأخِّراً، فأنصتَ جيداً لأنينِ رغبتِها آخرَ الليل؛ حيثُ صارتْ الشجرةُ في الصباحِ التالي خزانةً رائعةً مليئةً بكلِّ ألوانِ الثيابِ.

كتابةٌ ثانية

ليسَ لأنّ بستانياً عجوزاً نسيَ سُترتَهُ مُعلّقةً على غصنِها ذاتَ مساءٍ، ليس لأنّه أثارَ رغبتَها الكامنةَ في أنْ تُزهرَ معاطفَ وشالاتِ حريرٍ، فقط لأن نَجّاراً نَزِقاً أنصتَ جيداً لأنينِ رغبتِها حينَ مرَّ متأخراً ذاتَ مساءٍ؛ فصارتْ الشجرةُ الحالمةُ في الحديقةِ النائيةِ خزانةً جميلةً مُكَدَّسةً بكلِّ ألوانِ الثياب.

THE TREE NOBODY UNDERSTOOD

First Writing

When he forgot his coat on the branch of a lonely tree
in a sad forest the old gardener did not suspect he would
provoke its perennial bewilderment and insistent need
to weave itself into the astonishment of its passersby,
and be a singular tree that blooms coats, garments
of many colors, and silk scarves lovers pick while
sleepily meandering under its sleepy shadow.
A mischievous carpenter walked through the forest
intently listening in the wee hours to the moan of
the tree's wish: in the morning it became a magnificent
wardrobe full of all colors of clothes.

Second Writing

It's not because an old gardener forgot his jacket hanging
on its branch one evening, it's not because he aroused its
unspoken wish to bloom coats and silk scarves, it's just
because a mischievous carpenter listened intently to the moan
of its wish when he walked by it one evening that the dreamy
tree in the forlorn garden became a beautiful wardrobe
stuffed with all colors of clothes.

شجيرةُ الحجارةِ

في عصرِ يومٍ من حياةٍ لمْ تبدأ بعدُ، يعثرُ طفلٌ على حجرٍ غريبٍ، فيَضعُهُ في إناءِ الماءِ، وينساه. في الصباحِ سيبحثُ عنهُ فلا يجدُهُ؛ غيرَ أنّهُ لنْ يربُطَ بينَ الحجرِ المُبتلِّ وشجيرةِ وَردٍ نبتتْ جِوارَ الإناءِ المسكوبِ، ولنْ يهتمَّ أحدٌ غير الطائرِ العَطِشِ، والذي جفَلَ حينَ سكبَ الإناءَ فنبضَ القلبُ الحجريُّ. قلبُ العاشقِ والذي صارَ حجَراً حينَ غادرْتِهِ، والآنَ شجيرة وردٍ سيقطفُها الولدُ الصغيرُ حينَ يكبرُ، ويضعُها في المزهريّةِ، المزهريّةُ التي كانت ذاتَ يومٍ قلبَكِ قبلَ أنْ نفترقَ، وأمّا الطائرُ فسيكملُ ذهولَهُ بعيداً عن قِصّتنا التي لمْ تعُدْ حتّى تهمُّنا نحن.

STONE SAPLING

In the afternoon of a day from a life that hasn't yet started
a child finds a strange stone, puts it into a pot of water
and forgets about it. He looks for it in the morning without
finding it, but doesn't connect the wet stone and the rose
sapling growing beside the spilled pot no one had paid
attention to except the thirsty bird who froze when it tipped
the pot over and the stone heart started beating.
The lover's heart, which turned to stone when you left,
and now the rose sapling, will be picked up by the boy
when he grows up and put in a vase, the vase that was
once your heart before we parted ways, and as for
the bird it'll go on astonished, far from our story
that no longer interests anyone, not even us.

ملائكةٌ قُدامَى

البناتُ الصغيراتُ يَنمْنَ باكراً لتَسيلَ شعورُهنّ عنِ الوسائدِ، تبلِّلُ أقدامَ ملائكةٍ حُفاةٍ، طوالَ الليلِ يَملئونَ الجِرارَ أغنياتٍ ليشربَ مُتعَبو النهارِ. البناتُ الصغيراتُ لا يكنسْنَ العتبةَ بعدَ المغيبِ، حيثُ تسَّاقطُ ضحكاتُ الحفاةِ فيصيرُ البيتِ شيئاً فشيئاً جَنَّةً صغيرةً مؤقّتةً. البناتُ الصغيراتُ لا يغزلْنَ في الليلِ أبداً كنزاتِهنّ؛ حيثُ يمكنُ لإبرةٍ عاثرةِ الحظِّ أنْ تَثقُبَ جرّةَ الملاكِ فتمطرُ السماءُ أطفالاً ذكوراً حَمقَى. البناتُ الصغيراتُ كُنَّ قبلَ طلوعِ الصّباحِ ملائكةً قُدامَى.

ANGELS OF OLD

Little girls go to bed early so their hair flows over the pillows,
wetting the feet of barefoot angels filling urns all night with
songs for the day-worn to drink. Little girls don't sweep
the doorstep after sunset where the chuckles of the barefoot
fall one by one slowly turning their house into a tiny
momentary paradise. Little girls don't knit their sweaters
at night, because a stray needle can poke the angel's urn
and imbecilic boys rain down from the sky. Little girls
before the break of dawn were angels of old.

أرواحٌ ليلية

الثيابُ المهملةُ في الليلِ تخرجُ،
تَجولُ في الغرفِ الباردةِ،
ترتدي كلماتِ أصحابها،
تحبُ، تكرهُ، تصرخُ،
تعودُ لتنامَ قبل طلوعِ الضجيج.
الثيابُ أرواحُنا المكبوتةُ في العتمة، في النسيانِ.
في الأرقِ الصاعدِ من تحديقِنا في السقوفِ،
في الخُطى مكومةً على عتباتِ البيوتِ مثل أوراقِ خريفٍ مطرودٍ
من المحبة.
الثيابُ كنوزُ الحنينِ إلى زمنٍ لا يعود،
وأغنياتٍ لا تنسى.
لا تتركوا الخِزانةَ في الليلِ مفتوحةً،
كي ترقدَ بسلامٍ أرواحُكمُ القديمةُ المعذبة.

NOCTURNAL SPIRITS

Discarded clothes come out at night,
they roam around in cold rooms,
wearing the words of their owners,
they love, they hate, they scream,
they go back to sleep before the rising racket.
Clothes are our spirits pent up in the dark, in forgetfulness.
In the sleeplessness emanating from our staring at the ceilings,
in the footsteps, heaped at the thresholds of homes like
autumn leaves banished from love.
Clothes, the troves of longing for a time that won't return,
and songs that can't be forgotten.
Don't leave the closet open at night,
your old tormented souls have to rest in peace.

أحلامٌ مُشوَّهةٌ

منذُ متى وأنتَ ترمي سمكاً في النهرِ ليصدِّقَ النهرُ نفسَهُ، ويكفَّ عن تسلّقِ الشرفاتِ؟ تُعَبّدُ كلَّ يومٍ شارعاً فلا تتعثرُ ذاكرةُ أصدقائكَ الموتى، توقظُ وسائدَ الدهشةِ من نومِها، تفكُّ رباطَ الخيلِ في لوحةِ الحائطِ المُملَّةِ، تُطَيِّرُ طائراتٍ ورقيّةٍ في سماءِ فكرتِكَ الضيِّقةِ. منذُ متى أنتَ لم تَبُحْ مرّةً برائحةِ مَن ضاجعَتْكَ في انقطاعِ الكهرباءِ؟ لمْ تَحْكِ أبداً عن تَجَهّمِ كفِّكَ اليُسرى لكفِّكَ اليُمنَى، عن سرقاتِكَ الشريفةِ لنبيذِ دعائِها في صلاةِ الفجرِ. قُلْ أيَّ شيءٍ الآنَ قبلَ أن تلدَ السعادةُ قاتلِيها، ويزهرَ شجرُ الفُلفلِ عبرَ نظرتِكَ الساهِمةِ، قُلْ أيَّ شيءٍ ، فكلامُكَ الصموتُ سينتهي بحرقةٍ في القلبِ.

DISTORTED DREAMS

How long have you been throwing fish in the river, to make
the river believe itself and stop climbing balconies? You pave
a street every day, so the memory of your dead friends
doesn't trip. You wake the pillows of astonishment from
their slumber, you untie the horse from the dull painting
on the wall, you fly kites in the sky of your narrow mind.
How long has it been that you haven't once revealed the scent
of a woman who slept with you during the blackout?
You never spoke of your left palm's scowl at your right,
about the nobility of your theft of the wine of supplication at
the dawn prayer. Say something now before joy gives birth
to its killers, before peppers bloom through your vacant gaze,
say something, before your mute words end in heartbreak.

ملائكةٌ صغار

في ليلةِ القدرِ
على سطحِ البيتِ حين هرعنا سراعاً كي نشاهدَ الملائكةَ لم نرَ شيئاً،
في صباحاتِنا التالية كنا نحكي عن ملائكةٍ صافحتنا،
بأجنحةٍ كبيرةٍ، وريشٍ أبيض،
تناولوا معنا السحور، مسحوا على رؤوسِنا بماءِ البركة،
والكبارُ أكملوا كذباتِنا بضحكاتٍ ملونةٍ بحزنٍ شفيف.
في تلك الأيامِ على سطحِ البيتِ نسينا هناك شيئاً لن نجده فيما بعد،
نسينا أطفالاً لم يكبروا أبداً،
لم يكذبوا أبداً،
نسينا هناك ملائكةَ حياتِنا.

LITTLE ANGELS

On the Night of Destiny on the roof of the house when we rushed to witness the angels we saw nothing, the mornings after we'd tell of angels who shook our hands, with big wings and white feathers, they ate the pre-dawn meal with us, wiped our hair with the water of blessing and the grown-ups played along with our lies with laughter tinged by consuming sorrow. As for those days on the roof of the house we forgot something there we'll never find again, we forgot children who never grew up, who never lied, we forgot
there the angels of our lives.

بيت يُشبهُ ضحكتَكَ

١

كان يقصُّ عليَّ أحسنَ القصصِ، ويرمي وردةَ قلبِه في الماءِ، يتلو على الصمتِ آياتِهِ ويَصفوْ كأنْ لمْ يكنْ قبلَهُ من حياةٍ، النهرُ الذي رافقَهُ في نزهةِ العَصرِ لمْ يكنْ واحداً، كانَ سُلالةً مِنْ قصائدَ، والبيتُ المشابهُ ضحكَتَهُ يقطنُ في الناحيةِ الأخرى من النومِ الخفيفِ، اثنينِ كنّا ولمْ نجدْ لنا ثالثاً غيرَ سُلَّمٍ للتنهّداتِ قبلَ أنْ يُراصِفَ كلَّ ليلةٍ أَوْبَتَهُ جِواري. كانَ يَقُصُّ عليَّ أحسنَ القصصِ حين انتبهتُ لأثرِ بكائهِ على الرملِ وبعدها لمْ أجدْني.

٢

أنتَ من أجلستَ قَلبي عَلى رُكبَتيكَ يومَ كانَ طائراً، وعَلى كَتِفَيكِ حِينَ كانَ بُندُقِيّة، ولمْ تُلقِهِ في النَّهرِ حَتى حِينَ صارَ قَلبِي حَجراً. أبِي يا ظِلَّ الشَّجرةِ الوَحِيدةِ فِي كَفِّ الطَّريق، الطَّريقِ التي وزَّعَت دُموعَها على المَارِّينَ بِعدالَةٍ كامِلةٍ، الطَّريقِ التي لَمْ يَعْبُرْ شُرُودَها سِواي.

A HOUSE THAT LOOKS LIKE YOUR LAUGH

1

He used to tell me the best stories, and throw the rose of his heart in the water, recite his verses to silence, and find serenity like no life before, the river accompanying him on his afternoon walk wasn't one, it was a lineage of poems, and the house that looked like his laughter lived on the other side of light sleep, we were two, no third but a ladder of sighs before his return, tucked in next to me every night. He used to tell me the best stories when I noticed a trace of his crying on the sand and after that I could no longer find myself.

2

You're the one who sat my heart on your knees the day
it was a bird, and on your shoulders when it was a rifle,
and you didn't throw it in the river even when my heart
turned to stone. Father, O shadow of the only tree in the
palm of the road, the road that apportions tears to passersby
with perfect justice, the road whose vagrancy only I traversed.

٣

أَعرفُ أنكَ كنتَ جندياً يومَ وُلدتُ، ولكنْ لماذا حمَلْتَنِي مِثلَ بندقيّةٍ؟

٤

الطفلُ العالقُ بيدكَ يا أبي، فَرِحاً كبالونةِ عيدٍ، صارَ أباً، تَعْلَقُ بيده الكلماتُ الحزينةُ.

٥

حينَ عُدتَ من العملِ مُرهقاً ونسيتَها يا أبي، لمْ أكرهْكَ، لكنّي كرهتُ الشيكولاتةَ.

3

I know you were a soldier the day I was born,
but why did you carry me like a rifle?

4

The child caught in your hand, O Father, joyous as a
festive balloon, became a father, sad words clinging
to his hand.

5

When you came back from work tired, and you forgot it,
Father, it wasn't you I hated, it was the chocolate.

٦

أَرُدُّ على هاتفكَ بفرحٍ، أُخبرُ أصدقاءَكَ الذين لمْ يعرفوا بغيابِكَ،
غادرْتَنا يا أبي؛ لكنَّ هاتفَكَ ما زالَ يرنُّ.

٧

لطالما ظننتُ أنَّ الظلالَ جدرانٌ تسيلُ مِنَ التعبِ،
وأنَّ قلبكَ ظِلٌّ مُتعبٌ لجدارٍ غائبٍ.

6

I answer your phone joyfully, tell your friends who didn't
know of your absence — you left us, O Father,
but your phone still rings.

7

I always thought shadows were walls dissolving from
exhaustion, and that your heart was the worn-out
shadow of an absent wall.

غيابٌ مبكر

لم يكن الوقتُ كافياً لتعلّمِ العزفَ مثل خطاكِ وهي تصعدُ درجَ البيت،
أو الغناءِ المقفى وأنت تغسلين الهواءَ من تعبِ الحنين،
لم يكن الوقتُ كافياً لزراعةِ الزهورِ بألوانِ ثيابكِ في أصصِ الوصايا،
وطلاءِ كلّ هذه الأبوابَ مثل شالِكِ بالأبيض البري،
ولا حتى لجزِ العشبِ في الممرات ليبدو كأنه استيقظَ على عجلٍ
كي يراكِ،
لم يكن الوقتُ كافياً لنشرحَ للنوافذِ أسبابَ هطولِ القرآنِ في
صباحٍ مبكر،
ولماذا جلبَ الجيرانُ كراسيَّهم معهم،
وكلماتِ العزاء في جيوبهم،
نثروها ملحاً على العتبات،
ولم يكن في البيتِ لا عصافيرَ،
ولا أمهات.

EARLY ABSENCE

Not enough time to learn how to play an instrument that
sounds like your steps climbing the stairs at home, or sing
rhyming songs as you wash air from the fatigue of longing,
not enough time to plant flowers the color of your clothes
in the hanging pots of testament, and paint all these doors
the untamed white of your scarf, nor even enough time
to cut the grass in the hallways and make it seem like it just
woke up in a hurry to see you, not enough time for us to
explain to the windows the Reasons and Occasions as
to why the Quran descended like rain one early morning,
why the neighbors brought their chairs with them, and words
of condolence in their pockets, which they scattered
like salt on the thresholds, while at home
there were neither birds, nor mothers.

كعكةٌ على شكلِ قلبٍ

١

في يومِ مولدي أشتري كعكةً على شكلِ قلبٍ،
كلما اشتريتُ واحدةً أتذكرُ «أنا صانعُ تورتات»
قصيدةَ «باسم النبريص» فابتسمُ.
أتذكرُ أنّه صَنعَ المئاتِ منها، ولمْ يَذقْ واحدةً؛
فسُكَّرُهُ لا يسمحُ . . .
حينَها أضعُ ابتسامتي مع النقودِ، وأَخرُجُ
حاملاً بين يديَّ قلباً يَرتجُّ.

٢

الأولادُ شَطروا القلبَ بينهم،
أخذوا حصَّتَهم مِنهُ،
القطعةُ التي لمْ يرغبْ بها أحدٌ،
تركْتُها للقصيدةِ.

٣

قلبُنا المحفورُ على الشجرةِ
يتسلّقُهُ النملُ والنسيانُ.

HEART-SHAPED CAKE

1

On my birthday I buy a cake shaped like a heart,
every time I buy one I remember "I'm a pie-maker,"
a poem by Bassem al-Nebrees, and I smile.
I remember he made hundreds but never tasted one —
his blood sugar wouldn't let him . . .
Then I took my smile out with the change and left
carting in my hands a swinging heart.

2

The kids split the heart between them
taking their share from it —
the piece no one wanted
I kept for the poem.

3

Our heart engraved on the tree
ants and forgetfulness climb all over.

٤

جهازُ رسمِ القلبِ يقولُ:
قلبٌ مستقيمٌ قلبٌ ميتٌ.

٥

حين يقفُ نعرفُ حظَّنا،
حيثُ طوالَ الوقتِ يَرفُّ القلبُ كعُملةٍ معدنيّةٍ.

4

Electrocardiogram says:
straight heart dead heart.

5

The heart flutters along like a spinning coin,
and we know our lot only when it stops.

مديحُ الهواءِ

لا تُنصِت إلى مديحِ الهواءِ لثيابكَ، قُلْ إنّها تنهّدات قديمةٌ يُردِّدُها المكانُ، لأُناسٍ عبَرُوه مسرعينَ، ولَمْ يلحقُوا بشيءٍ. لا تُنصِت إلى مديحِ الهواءِ لروايةٍ أشدَّ غموضاً من ذاكرةِ قوسِ قزحَ هارباً من شجارِ الغيومِ، يُفتّشُ عن ألوانِه في قميصِكَ المُشَجَّرِ بالغناءِ. أنتَ الذي عبَرَ السريرةَ بوسامةِ الحُبِّ، والمكانُ بائعُ حلوَى يغزلُ ما لا يفهمُه المارّةُ من عتابِ الحياةِ، البراءاتُ غادرَتْ ثيابكَ خِلسةً، وارتقتْ لسماءٍ بعيدةٍ. خارجاً عنِ النصِّ اخلعْ بابَك الخشبيَّ من صريرِه، وحذاءَك مِنْ رُهابِ الطريقِ، ولا تُنصِتْ إلى مديحٍ كهذا، وامضِ عارياً: هواءٌ يمدحُه الهواءُ.

THE FLATTERY OF AIR

Don't listen to air flattering your clothes, take it as old sighs
the place repeats for people who pass through quickly and
never catch anything. Don't listen to air flattering a tale more
inscrutable than the memory of a rainbow fleeing scuffling
clouds, in search of its colors in your shirt forested in song.
You're the one who traverses inner being with love's grace,
and place is a candy-seller spinning whatever passersby
don't get from life's reproach, innocence furtively takes
leave from your clothes and rises to a distant sky.
Going off script, yank your wooden door out of
its creaks, and your shoes from the phobia
of the road—and don't listen to this kind
of flattery, go naked, air flattered by air.

معراج

. . . وصاعدٌ درجَ الروحِ بلا وجهٍ، أو قناع، أُطيِّرُ نحو الله أغنيةً سرقتُها من حقلِ أمنيات، عارياً ندماً، خفيفاً أُبسملُ المحبةَ فيصير الليلُ مساجدَ، والاحلامُ وسائدَ، أُرنِّمُ الرضا للصمتِ، للشرفة النائمة، ولي، صاعدٌ درجَ الروحِ، أتنفّسُ مثلَ الاشجارِ كلماتَ النورِ، يتَرجِمُني الصمتُ أهِلّةً، فيصير الهمسُ عناقيد، والكلماتُ حدائق، وليس يصحَبُني سواي. أنا المشْتَمِلُ بأنك تبسِمُ لي وكأنّك لم تخلُق غيري، أنك تعرفني ذنباً وبكاء، أنا المستدفئ قلبي بالمِسكِ وبَخُور رضاك حين أذِنتَ لاسمك يتنزه منفرداً في قلبي، أن أدخل جنتك الكبرى من باب قِصار السُّوَر، فأنا حين وصلت إلى أعتاب الروح، لمستُ البابَ، بابَك يا صانع روحي.

ASCENSION

Ascending the staircase of the soul without face or mask,
I fly a song I stole from the field of wishes toward God,
with no regrets at all, weightless, I intone love so nights
become mosques, and dreams pillows, I sing contentment
to silence, to the sleeping balcony, and to me, ascending
the stairs of the soul, I breathe like trees the words of light,
the silence translates me into crescents, then whispers become
clusters, words gardens, and I am my only companion.
I am the one your smile embraced as if you had created
no one else, the one you know as guilt and tears, I am
the one whose heart basks in the musk and incense of your
favor when you allowed your name to wander around alone
in my heart, to enter your great paradise through the gate of
the short Chapters, when I reached the thresholds of the soul,
I touched the door, your door, O Maker of my soul.

مقاطع قصيرة

١

الطيورُ تخافُ تحطُّ
حين تَعبرُ قلبي،
تَخافُ تأكلُ خبزَ أحزانِه
فتصيرُ قلباً مِثلَهُ
وتموت.

٢

للظلّ ذاكرةُ أسَى
تُمرّرُها الجدرانُ من بيتٍ لبيت؛
حتّى إذا ما مرّ بِي ظلّي
أراني دونما أدري بكيت!

SMALL FRAGMENTS

1

The birds are scared to perch
when passing my heart —
afraid they'd eat the bread of its sorrow,
and become, like it, a heart,
and die.

2

Shadow holds a memory of sadness
walls pass it on from home to home;
and when my shadow passes me by
I find myself crying out of nowhere!

٣

البيوتُ في الحرب يأكلُهَا الحزنُ،
تكلّم نفسَها،
تمشي إلى البحر من ضجرٍ وحيدة،
وتعودُ تدفنُ رأسَها في زحامِ المدينة
البيوتُ في الحرب يجرحُها القَصفُ،
وكالناسِ.. تموت بالغرغرينا.

٤

حين أُعْطي لقيصرَ . . . ما لقيصر
وما للهِ . . . لله
ماذا تبقّى لي . . . ؟

٥

يا لها من شرفةٍ وجريدة،
وغسيلي المعلّقُ من ساعديه
تجلِدُه الريحُ
سينهار عاجلاً،
أم يحتمل . . . حتى نزيف القصيدة؟؟

3

Homes in war are eaten up by sorrow.
They talk to themselves,
restlessly making their way to the sea, alone,
and bury their heads in the crowds of the city.
In war, homes, like people, get injured by shelling,
and, like people . . . die of gangrene.

4

When I render unto Caesar . . . what is Caesar's
and unto God . . . what is God's —
What's left for me?

5

What a balcony and what a newspaper,
my laundry hanging from its sleeves
whipped by wind —
will it break down quickly,
or resist . . . until the poem bleeds out?

٦

حَلَمَ السرو بأنّ الغيمَ يغازله
فاشتاق إليه.
وأطال أطال اليدَ
لكنّ الغيمَ العابرَ
كان حبيبَ الجدول،
ونصيبَ الأرض.

٧

تذكّرتُ..
وسيارةُ الإسعاف تخرِقُ حاجزَ الصوت،
وجرحُكَ يرتجُّ دماً وصراخاً
أنّكَ — غير منظر الدماء —
تكرهُ السرعةَ الفائقة.

٨

— حين تنام ضَعْ كوباً من الماء جانبك.
— لِمَ يا أم . . . ؟؟
— ليشربَ الملاكُ حارسُك.

6

The cypress dreamt the cloud was flirting,
and so longed for it.
It reached and reached,
but the passing cloud
was the stream's lover,
and soil's fate.

7

It came back to me . . .
while the ambulance broke the sound barrier
and your wound trembled blood and screams,
that you — aside from the sight of blood —
hate excessive speed.

8

— When you go to bed, leave a glass of water by your side.
— Why, mother . . . ?
— So your guardian angel can drink.

٩

حلمتُ كأنّكَ وردةً في يدي،
وفي الصبحِ طالَ انتظاري . . .
فلا البابُ دقَّ،
ولا رنّ الهاتف!
حتّى المساءُ الذي جاءَ يغلقُ النافذة؛
كان منكسرَ البال، مكتفياً بالقصيدة!

١٠

ميتاً كنت، حين دُقَ البابُ
— منْ؟
قالتْ صورتي في الإطار.
قلتُ: هذا أنا . . . عدتُ أمسحُ عنك الغبار.

9

I dreamt you as a rose in my hand,
and waited the morning long . . .
no knock at the door
no ring of the phone!
Even nighttime come to shut the window
had its spirit broken, content with the poem.

10

I was dead when there was a knock on the door
— who? said my image in the frame —
I said: it's me . . . back to dust you off.

تأملات

١

فيما مضى كان للشعراءِ أصبعٌ سادسةٌ في كلّ يد
لتحتملَ اليدُ وجعَ الكتابةِ.
كان لهم ثلاثُ حواسٍ إضافية
لقراءةِ الغيب وفهمِ لغةِ النحلِ ومداواةِ العشاق.
ولم يكن لديهم أيَّ شيءٍ في موضعِ القلب
ليعبروا وجعَ الحياةِ بلا موتٍ مبكر.

٢

أكفُّنا كل صباح تواظبُ على غسيلِ الدماءِ بإخلاصٍ وصمت،
ونحنُ نواظبُ كل ليلةِ ترويضَها كي تصيرَ سكاكين.

٣

الطفلُ الذي غادرَنا نائماً ساعةَ القصف،
لماذا نَسِيَ رائحةَ وجهِهِ على الوسادة؟

MEDITATIONS

1

In times past, poets had a sixth finger on each hand
to better endure the ache of writing. They had three
extra senses, to read the unknown, understand
the language of bees, and heal lovers.
They had nothing in place of a heart
to traverse the pain of life except early death.

2

Our palms meticulously wash blood each morning
in silence and with great devotion, and every night we
diligently train them into knives.

3

The sleeping child who left us at the hour of shelling,
why did he forget the smell of his face on the pillow?

٤

حياةٌ مثل موتٍ مقلوب،
كما إن الجبلَ محضُ حفرةٍ مقلوبة.

٥

الجورب الوحيد، والذي فقدَ رفيقَه يفكرُ في امرأةٍ بساقٍ واحدة.

٦

تقولُ البئرُ: ما حاجتي للبكاء!
كلي دمعٌ، وعيني واحدة!

٧

لست حزيناً ، لكني أكتب،
وهذا يُذكرُني بالأشياءِ المحزنة.

4

Life is like an upside-down death,
just like a mountain is an upside-down pit.

5

The lone sock that lost its mate
thinks of a one-legged woman.

6

The well says: Why should I cry!
I'm all tears, and one eye!

7

I'm not sad, but I'm writing,
and this reminds me of sad things.

٨

لماذا يهربُ الصفاءُ خلسةً بسلةِ أحلامِنا،
فلا تعد شمسٌ واحدةٌ تعبثُ بشَعْرِ صباحِنا اليتيم؟
لماذا لا غيمةً نائمةً تتوسدُ ضحكةَ الحديقة؟
أو تمررُ فاكهةَ البكاءِ على أعينِ الحنين؟
لماذا نغذُّ الخطى على طرقٍ ميتة،
ولا يصلُ الشهيقُ حتى إلى آخر القلب؟
لماذا يتخثرُ في دمي دمُ المدينة،
والكلمات يصرعُها رهابٌ صموت؟

٩

الصيادُ يباهي نفسَه بما حدث، والفخُ يباهي نفسَه بما حدث،
وحده الطائرُ في الفخِ عليه أن يسمعَ روايتين كاذبتين،
ويهزُ لهما رأسَ الندم.

8

Why does clarity abscond with our basket of dreams,
so that not a single sun is left to play with the hair of our
orphan morning? Why doesn't a sleepy cloud cushion
itself in the garden's laughter? Or parade the fruit of
weeping before the eye of longing?
Why do we pick up the pace on dead roads,
when breathing in doesn't reach the bottom of the heart?
Why does the blood of the city curdle in my blood,
and words deaden in quiet dread?

9

The hunter brags about what happened,
and the trap also brags about what happened,
only the bird in the trap has to listen to two tall tales,
and shake its head in regret.

١٠

راعي الفراغَ يبدُ أغنامَه،
يخطُ على الرملِ شكلَ أظلافِها لتدلَّهُ على الماء،
وعلى الماءِ أسماءَها لَتضِلّهُ عن الوقت.
يُمسدُ فراءَ الحنينِ بما تيسر من أصابعِ النسيان،
يحلبُ بين كفيه طولَ النهارِ ضرعَ التذكُّرِ،
حتى إذا أتى الليلُ أشعلَ نايه،
ونامَ وحيداً،
تاركاً قطيعَه لذئبِ البكاء.

١١

في البدء كانت الظلالُ أسرع منا قليلاً،
ثم صارت ترافقُنا،
الآن نجرُ الظلالَ خلفَنا مثل أكياسٍ مكدسةٍ بالأمنيات الميتة.

10

The shepherd of the void scatters his sheep,
tracing in the sand the shape of their hoofs to guide him
to water, and on the water their names to stray from time.
He strokes the fleece of yearning with all the fingers of
forgetfulness he can muster, milking all day between
his palms the udder of remembrance, so when night comes,
he lights his flute, and sleeps alone,
leaving his flock to the wolf of the cry.

11

At the beginning shadows were a little faster than we were,
then they walked with us, now we drag the shadows
like sacks stuffed with dead wishes.

١٢

قال الأطفالُ لعبنا ولكن أبداً لم نفرح،
قال الشجرُ أكملنا اخضرارَنا وأبداً لم نثمر،
والجرسُ يقولُ أرقصُ في عراءِ السكينةِ وحدي،
ويقولُ الكلامُ لم يعد لديَّ ما أقولُه كي ينتبهَ الغيابُ لي ويغيب.
الأطفالُ والشجرُ والجرسُ وضعوا في النهرِ قارباً من ورقِ النسيان،
قالوا: أيها الغرقُ خُذ وصايانا بعيداً، بعيداً
نحن كَبِرنا ولم يعدْ من جدوى لشيء.

١٣

أَرِقٌ كساعةِ حائطٍ معطلة،
لا يبصرُها أحد،
ترقبُ العابرين،
كي تعرفَ الوقت.

١٤

قال لي:
طرفي الصناعي الجديد لا يصلح لشيء؛
كنت أوقدُ ناراً للشاي بساقي الخشبية إذا لزم الأمر.

12

The kids said we played but never rejoiced, the trees said
we turned completely green but never bore fruit, the bell says,
I dance alone in barren calm, speech says, I have nothing more
to say for absence to notice me and go away. The children,
the trees, and the bell put a boat made of forgetfulness paper
in the river, they said, Ahoy, you there drowning, take our
wills and testament far, far away. We've gotten older,
and now it all feels pointless.

13

Sleepless like a broken clock on the wall,
unseen by anyone, watching passersby,
to tell the time.

14

He told me:
My new artificial limb is good for nothing,
if it came to that I'd make a fire for tea with my wooden leg.

١٥

البائعُ المتجولُ ظلَّ طوالَ النهارِ ينادي على بضاعته،
ولم يشترِ أحد.
ظل ينادي: نكاتٌ للبيع، نكاتٌ جديدةٌ طازجة.
دارَ في القريةِ كلّها شارعاً .. شارعاً، ولم يشترِ أحد،
دقَّ على الأبوابِ، النوافذِ، والجدرانِ، ولم يشترِ أحد.
واحدٌ فقط اشترى نكتةً واحدة، ولم يضحكْ؛
لم يرغب أن يرى قريته حزينةً هكذا.

١٦

البحيرةُ نائمةٌ!!
فَسرْ لي إذن دوائرَ ضحكتِها بعد حصاةِ الايقاظ،
بريدَ رسائِلها غمازاتِ وأغاني،
إوزَتا نهديها اللتان على وشكِ الفرارِ!
فَسرْ . . . فَسرْ . . .
ولا تَقلْ إنَّ بعضَ النومِ إثم.

15

The peddler has been out hawking his wares all day
and no one is buying. He keeps hawking: jokes for sale,
fresh new jokes. He went around the village street by street
and no one was buying, he knocked on doors, windows,
and walls, and no one was buying.
Only one bought a single joke, and didn't laugh:
he didn't want to see his village so sad.

16

The lake is asleep!!
Explain to me then the circles of her laughter after the pebble
of awakening, the messages of her letters made of dimples
and songs, the geese of her breast about to flee!
Explain . . . explain . . .
And don't say that some sleep is a sin.

١٧

مدَّ الليلُ صنارةً إلى قلبي، فغرستُها.
وقلتُ: خذهُ إلى أي أرضٍ تشاء.
حتى تغيبَ عنه الأسئلة، ويفيضَ منه الغناء.

١٨

لو قلتَ لي تعال لجئتُ،
ولو قلتَ لي إبتعد.
لكنك أطلقتَ لي عَنانَ الحياة، أركضُ في خُيلاءِ العدم، أشربُ حيرةَ الاشتهاء،
لا شيء لي، ولي كل شيء.
لو قلتَ لي تعالَ، فأملأُ صوتي أغاني.
لو قلت لي إبتعد، أفتت وقتي ندماً ولكن،
لم تقل يا رب لي،
وكل الذي أنتظرهُ علامة.

17

The night threw a hook to my heart, I planted it.
And I said: take it to any land you wish.
So questions go missing, and the singing brims over.

18

If you told me come I would,
and so if you told me go —
But you unleashed life on me,
I race about the specters of the void, I sip
the bewilderment of desire, nothing for me,
everything for me. If you told me come,
I'd fill my voice with song. If you told me
stay away, I'd rip my time to pieces
in regret, but you didn't, O Lord,
and all I'm waiting for is a sign.

١٩

يطيرُ نحو الأرضِ،
لا يرفُ له جناح، لا يبصرُ الهاوية،
فارغاً من التعبِ، مثقلاً بالطمأنينةِ، بالنظرة الوادعة،
بالرصاصةِ الصغيرة جداً في القلب.
طائرٌ يطيرُ نحو الأرض.

٢٠

زوج جوارب
طائرين سكارى
تعلقا بحبل غسيل.

19

Flying toward the ground, not flapping a wing,
not seeing the abyss, hollowed out from fatigue,
heavy with serenity, a gentle gaze,
and with a tiny bullet in its heart.
A bird flying toward the ground.

20

A pair of socks
two drunken birds
caught on a clothesline.

أثرُ فراشتكَ

كان عليَّ أنْ أعرفَ منذُ زمنٍ بعيدٍ لماذا لا أتحملُ أعمالَ «درويش» الكاملةَ في مكتبتي. درجاتُ البيتِ مهترئةٌ نعمْ؛ لكنّها حميمةٌ. لونُ الطلاءِ باهتٌ؛ غَيرَ أنّه ليسَ من درجاتِ الأخضرِ الساذجِ، بناتُ الجيرانِ الصغيراتِ يغنينَ نشازاً طيلةَ القيلولةِ؛ غيرَ أنّهنَّ يهربنَ حينَ أصحو. فقطْ ديوانُ «درويش» هو ما يستفزُّني تماماً بنصفِ تلكَ الابتسامةِ الذابلةِ على الغِلافِ، بنظّارتِه المُحايدةِ وشَعرِهِ الناعمِ دونَ أيِّ مناسبةٍ، بلا مبالاتِهِ بي كشاعرٍ وصاحبِ بيتٍ، يستفزُّني بضرورتِه الحتميّةِ في الواجهةِ؛ حتى لا يُلمِّح أصدقائي إلى غَيرتي مِنه. ثُمَّ إنّه أكثرُ الكتبِ بدانةً في المكتبةِ مما يجعلُ من غجريّةِ «خالد جمعة» مِثلَ دعوةِ زفافٍ.

غيرَ أنَّ كلَّ هذا لا يعدِلُ غضبي منهُ حينَ تَترك الفراشةُ كلَّ المكتبةِ، وتقفُ على حافتِهِ لِتصفّقَ له.

THE TRACE OF YOUR BUTTERFLY

It's been a while since I've wanted to figure out why
I can't stand Darwish's *Complete Works* in my library.
Yes, the stairs of the house are shabby, but there's a warmth
to them. The color of the paint has faded, but it isn't that
homely shade of green, the neighbor's little girls sing off tune
all afternoon, but run away when I wake up from my nap.
It's only Darwish's collection of poetry that provokes
everything in me, with that withering smirk on the dust jacket,
his eyeglasses that take no sides, and his unreasonably straight
hair, his utter disregard for me as a poet, as a home owner,
he irks me with his unavoidable presence at the entrance,
just so my friends can't hint at my jealousy, on top of it
being the thickest book in the library, making Khaled Juma's
Gypsy Woman look like a wedding invitation.
All this doesn't even come close to my anger at him
when the butterfly ignores the whole library and
stands on the edge of the book to applaud him.

مكنسة الخراب

قبل نهوضِ الصباحِ يسكرُ الحُلمُ، يفرُّ منْ نافذتي، يُراودُ شوارعَ ولغةً عن نفسِها.

حُلمي الهاربُ كان طوالَ النهارِ مُتَّكئاً على مشهدِ صمتي، أدجّنُ فكرةً بريّةً أنَّ المدنَ نساءٌ تعضُّ آباءَها في سكرةِ الجنسِ، وتَحبلُ بسياسيينَ وكَتبَةٍ. يسكرُ الحُلْمُ تماماً في ظلمةٍ لا ترَى حتى نفْسَها، فيما التاريخُ مُضَّجعٌ يُنقِّي شهيقَه من غبارِ الحروبِ، ويلقي في سلّةِ المهملاتِ بأوطانٍ قديمةٍ. يسيلُ الحُلْمُ كسائلٍ منَويٍّ يفتشُ عن وجودِه المنتظِر بشغفٍ وصمتٍ، المدينةُ تباعدُ ما بينَ ساقيها لهَذَرِ أحلامي، تهزُّها الدهشةُ الأولى.

المدينةُ والتي على وشكِ أنْ تصبحَ مُدناً، تتكاثرُ في سماءِ ليلِها، ثُمّ تنهارُ موقِنةً باكتمالِ الخصوبةِ. كلُّ شيءٍ عاهرٌ في الساعةِ الأخيرةِ قبلَ طُلوعِ الصباحِ، كلُّ شيءٍ مُبَلَّلٌ بالخطيئةِ ومُتَّشِحٌ بالذنوبِ، عاثرٌ بالحجارةِ كشارعٍ لمْ يعبِّدْهُ الخليفةُ، ولم تَكنُسْهُ يدُ الخرابِ. كلُّ شيءٍ يُمسكُ الوقتَ مِنْ خصيتِه في الساعةِ التي تسبقُ النهارَ الجميلَ.

HAVOC'S BROOM

Before morning wakes up, the dream gets drunk, escapes
through my window, and proceeds to seduce streets and
language. My fugitive dream leans on the scene of my silence
all day, I tame the wild idea that cities turn into women
biting their fathers in the heat of sex and get pregnant
with politicians and writers. The dream gets hammered
in a darkness that can't even see itself, while history lies in
bed clearing its lungs from the dust of war, tossing ancient
homelands into the trash. The dream flows like semen
in search of its awaited existence with zeal and silence,
the city spreads its legs to the babble of my dream,
and quivers at the first wonder.
The city — about to become cities — multiplies in the sky of
its night, then collapses, certain insemination was completed.
Everything in the late hours is promiscuous, all soaked
in sin and cloaked with guilt, tripping on stones like a street
the Caliph did not pave, and the hand of havoc did not sweep.
Everything holds time by the balls in the hour
preceding the beautiful day.

أطهو أنيني

في الليلِ يصنعُ اللّهُ الفقراءَ واللصوص والعاهرات،
يجبِلُهم من طينِ السخطِ وماءِ الرضا.
ينثرُهم حولَ خرافه اللاهية سياجاً من ذئاب.
القلبُ صكُ عتاب،
واليدُ تمسحُ عن الفمِ دمَ البراءة.
جميلون مثل رفاقِ الطفولة،
مرحون كحذاءٍ واسعٍ،
ورافعو رؤوسهم عالياً كأنهم علمُ البلاد.
في الليل يصنعني اللهُ على مهلٍ وأناة،
يحركُ في رأسي حِساءَ التذمر،
يذوبُ في القلبِ حصى كلماتِه البريئة،
يرشُ توابلَ الغناء.
في الليل يطهو اللهُ أنيني على صوتِ عبد الباسط،
ينثرُ على نهرِ أسئلتِه رمادي، فأطفو كحلمٍ لا تفسره يداي،
أبكي، يرقُ ليله لي ويضمني على مضضٍ يتيماً بلا بداية وليس لي انتهاء
الليلُ صار أبي، وصرت له كاتب الشكاية.
صار الليلُ أخي وصرت خائن النهار.

STEWING MY GROANS

At night, God makes the poor, the thieves, and the prostitutes,
molding them from the clay of wrath and the water
of acceptance. He scatters them around his distracted sheep
like a fence of wolves. The heart is a voucher for reproach,
and the hand wipes the blood of innocence from the mouth.
Beautiful as childhood friends, light-hearted as a wide shoe,
and their heads held high as if they were the country's flag.
At night, God makes me slowly and deliberately, stirring
in my head the stew of discontent, and in my heart he melts
the pebbles of his innocent words, sprinkling in the spice
of song. At night God stews my groan to the sound of
Abdul Basit, scattering over the river of his questions my
ashes, then I float like a dream my hands cannot interpret,
I cry, his night softens to me, begrudgingly he embraces me,
an orphan with no beginning, nor is there an end to me.
The night's become my father and to him I'm the Scribe of
Complaint. Night's become my brother and I, Traitor of Day.

حديقة الجنون

ينساكِ القلبُ، فتصاب الأمكنةُ بحُمّى حضورِكِ،
يذكركِ، فيرشحُ من ساعةِ الحائطِ عطرٌ مسمولُ العينين،
تلتفُ على معصمي الموسيقى مثل أفاعٍ حولَ أفاع.
لا أبنيةً تتراصفُ مثل الكلماتِ على بحر الرمل بعينيَّ،
لا آياتِ ترتعشُ على صوتِ المُقرئ قبلَ طلوعِ الفجرِ بقلبي،
لا شيءَ يصادفُ مرآةً واحدةً لم تتكسّر بعد.
ماءٌ أنتِ يفتّتُ حصاةَ الحنين، ويلوكُني.
هواءٌ من تعبٍ يَجزُّ ابتسامةَ موتكِ،
فأصيرُ عشباً لذاكرةِ طريقٍ لم نمشِهِ معاً.
كوني زَفيراً يمرِّرُ في قلبي إبرةَ النسيان، ويغزلُ ثوباً ضافياً لمساءِ
حضورِك.
كوني شَهيقاً يسرقُ البيوت من مشاغِلِها،
ويتركُ الشرفاتِ ساهمةً تُمَوِّلُ ياسمينَ صوتك.
صمتٌ أنتِ يفتِّتُ حصاةَ الوقتِ وينثرُني على مقربةٍ من وجهِكِ.
وجهُكِ الذي يهُزُّ كل ليلة ستائرَ نومي، فلا أنام.
مشوشةٌ تلكَ الطريق التي تقطعينَها تجاهي،
حيث لا مكانَ لي، لا وجهَ، لا مرايا تدل علي حواسِكِ المفعمة بالحب،
في حين يكثرُ الجنودُ، والموتى، وحاملو الأعلام المزيَّفة.
طريقي مشوشةٌ لذا كوني مثلَ البلادِ غامضة، مثل الوجوه غاضبة،
مثل هذه الأخطاء المتكاثرة في القلب؛
كي تجمعَنا ربما صدفةٌ واحدةٌ في حديقةِ الجنون.

THE GARDEN OF MADNESS

The heart forgets you, places catch the fever of your presence,
it remembers you, the clock on the wall seeps perfume with
languid eyes, music wraps around my wrist like snakes around
snakes. No buildings pack themselves together like words on
the sea of sand in my eyes, no verses tremble over the voice
of the one reciting before the coming of dawn in my heart, no thing
stumbles upon a mirror not yet shattered. You are water
crushing the pebbles of longing, gnawing on me.
The air of fatigue cuts the smile of your death, and I become
grass in the memory of a path we haven't walked together.
Be the breath out that threads the needle of forgetfulness through
my heart and knit an abundant garment for the evening of your
appearance. Be the breath in that robs the homes of their
worries, and leaves balconies dazed serenading the jasmine
of your voice. You are silence crushing the pebbles of time
and scattering me beside your face. Your face that every night
swells the curtains of my sleep, and I don't sleep. Muddled
is the path on which you cross toward me, where no place,
no face, no mirror, guides me to your senses brimming
with love, when soldiers, and the dead, and the bearers of false
flags proliferate. My path is muddled, so be like the country
inscrutable, like the faces irate, like these errors proliferating
in the heart; so we meet in the garden of madness
when luck strikes once.

سطوعُ العاديّةِ

١

أيُّ حكمةٍ في أنْ ينصبَ الصيّادُ فِخاخَهُ على شكلِ قصائدَ؟ أوْ أنْ يخلعَ البحرُ ثيابَه ليبدو ماجناً حين تعبرينَه؟ كيفَ لي أنْ أهجسَ باسمكِ قبلَ النومِ، ولا تسمعينَ صوتَ حنيني المُتسلِّقِ شُرفاتِكِ لَبلاباً وترانيمَ؟ أنا عَشّابُ حدائقِ صمتكِ، لصُّ مناديلكِ، والمسحورُ يُصلِّي كيْ يطلعَ صبحٌ مِنْ بينِ أصابعِكِ النسَّاجةِ عُشَّ عصافير. هاربٌ أنا مِنْ رحلةِ الشتاءِ والصيفِ، ظامِئةُ اليدينِ رايتي إليكِ، وقلبي يعَضُّ على كتابِ السرابِ، النارُ في صدري دفنَتْ رأسَها، وليسَ يعرفُ رأسيَ المقطوعَ في الشارعِ غيرُ الغُرباءِ.

RADIANCE OF THE ORDINARY

1

What wisdom is there in a hunter setting traps in the form
of poems? Or for the sea to strip naked and give airs of
impudence as you pass through it? How can I mumble your
name to myself before falling asleep, and you not hear my
longing scale your balcony as vines and hymns? I am the
herbalist of the gardens of your silence, the thief of your
scarves, and the bewitched praying for a morning that
rises from your fingers to weave a birds' nest. I escape
the caravan of winter and summer, the hands of my banner
thirst for you, and my heart is biting the book of mirage,
the fire in my chest buries its crown, and no one save
the strangers recognize my severed head on the street.

٢

أيُّ حكمةٍ في أنْ أبني لكِ بيتاً في الجَنَّةِ، ويسكُنُهُ الهواءُ؟! أوْ أنْ أقدَّ اشتياقي ولا شاهدَ غيرَ طريقٍ لا يؤدي إليكِ؟! أتنفّسُ وحدي الأغنياتِ: شهيقُ حوريّاتٍ، وزفيرُ ملائكةٍ، وأنتِ كفُّكِ تُلقِيني عُملةً معدنيّةً في سماءِ احتمالِكِ، وتلقَفُني ضاحكةً كلَّ ليلةٍ يدُ الألمِ. مِن يدي تفرُّ صحراءُ كاملةٌ، وتنتشي بين كُوفةِ القلبِ وبَصْرَتِهِ سوقَ نخّاسينَ. أجيبي رسولِيَ الحاملَ موتي إلى ماءِ الحياةِ، من ألْفِ لَيلةٍ اعطِني ليلةً يتَوَكّأُ قلبي عليها، ويرفعُها غيمةَ ذكرياتٍ، وخُذي ما لا أحدَ سَمِعَهُ، ولا أحدَ رآهُ غيرَ دمِ العاشقين.

2

What wisdom is there for me in building you a home in
paradise only to be inhabited by air? Or for me to split open
my desire with no witness but a path not leading to you?
I am the only one breathing songs: breathing in of nymphs
and breathing out of angels, and your hand tosses me like
a coin in the sky of your likelihood, while every night the hand
of pain, laughing, catches me. From my hand a whole desert
escapes and between the Kufa and the Basra of the heart
a slave market rejoices. Respond to my messenger carrying
my death to the water of life, from A Thousand Nights,
give me one night for my heart to lean on, and raise
as a cloud of memories, take what no one has heard,
and no one but for the blood of lovers seen.

ما لم أَقلـهُ لي

إلى صديقي رزق المزعنن

١

لو أَنّا نُطلقُ أصابِعَنا العَطشَى لتكوِّرَ من غيمِ الصيفِ قلائدَ ليتامَى الحُبِّ، لو أنَّ العَينَ تَمُدُّ بصيرتَها، ترمِي أيّاماً تالفةً في النهرِ وتصطادُ صباحاً لا يُوجعُنا. لو أنّا نشعلُ مِن حَطبِ الشوقِ ونولمُ أرغفةً تضحكُ للنارِ، حكاياتٍ تتزاورُ مِثلَ الجِيرانِ الحمقى، وبريداً يسكبُنا كالشايِ على طاولةِ الذِكرَى. تعالوا يا غُيّابَ القلبِ، نغنّي أغنيةً لا تَصدأُ، نسيّجُ نظرتَنا الأولى بحليبِ الزَهوِ، ونَبسمُ حين يرنُّ الهاتفُ في الليلِ ولا نسمعُ صوتاً. نلقي «لو أنّا» في كلِّ حديقةٍ؛ كي تزهرَ في العامِ القادمِ غاباتَ بكاءٍ.

WHAT I DIDN'T SAY TO ME

To my friend Rizk al Muza'nan

1

If we were to unleash our thirsty fingers to shape beaded
necklaces out of summer clouds for orphans of love, if the eye
were to extend its vision, cast expired days into the river,
and catch a morning that won't make us ache. If we were to
light a fire from the wood of longing, and hold a banquet of
loaves laughing to the fire, as well as stories visiting each other
like foolish neighbors, and mail that pours us out like tea
on the table of memory. Come here you absent of heart,
let's sing a song that doesn't rust, fence off our first gaze
with the milk of bluster, and smile when the phone rings
at night and we don't hear anything. We cast "If we were to"
into every garden, to bloom next year into forests of tears.

٢

لا شيءَ يشبهُ فكرتَنا المرتبِكةَ أكثرَ من غيمةِ صيفٍ، بيضاءَ، بعيدةٍ، مستوحشةٍ، ولا يمكنُ التعلّقُ بها. لا شيءَ يشبهُ جارتَنا العابرةَ أكثرَ من دُميةٍ قديمةٍ، رثّةِ الملابسِ، مبعثرةِ الشّعرِ، غارقةٍ في غبارِها، ولا نحاولُ التخلّصَ منها. لا شيءَ يشبهُ حارتَنا القديمةَ أكثرَ مِن حياتِنا الميّتةِ حين ندفّئُها عبثاً كدُميةٍ مُستوحشة، كغيمةٍ رثّةٍ، وحارةٍ نائمةٍ في ذاكرةٍ بيضاءَ. هذا لا يُسهّلُ عليكَ شعوركَ بأُلفةِ اليأسِ وموسيقى الدُوارِ، وأنتَ تعبرُ صباحاتِكَ المتكرِّرةَ كلَّ يومٍ، كل يوم.

٣

باتّجاهِ قلبِهِ الضالِّ مَدَّ أُلفَتَهُ المحنيَّةَ الظهرِ، هناك قريباً مِنْ سِدرةِ الشّكِّ وعصافيرِ التجلّي، في ظلالِ الهناءةِ القصيرةِ، والبَراحِ المُترامِي لوجعٍ لا يُعرفُ مَن صاحبُهُ، هناكَ حيثُ يَمرُّ بطيئاً أمامَ بصيرتِهِ نهرُ ندمٍ صغيرٍ، رمى حصواتِه السبعَ بكاملِ حسرتِهِ، بحنينٍ شاهقٍ لتجربةٍ لمْ يقترِفْها بعدُ،
ثمّ عادَ إلى شَكِّهِ الجميلِ خالي الوفاضِ مِن أيِّ يقينٍ كان.

2

Nothing looks like our befuddled idea more than a summer cloud, white, distant, lonely, that you can't get attached to. Nothing looks like our passing neighbor more than an old doll with tattered clothes, tangled hair, drowning in its dust, and we don't try to get rid of it. Nothing looks like our old neighborhood more than our dead life when for no reason we warm it up like a lonely doll, a tattered cloud, and a sleepy neighborhood in white memory. This doesn't make your familiarity with despair and the music of vertigo as you go through your repetitious mornings every day, every day, any easier.

3

In the direction of his stray heart, he stretched out his bent back, there near the Lote Tree of Doubt and the birds of epiphany in the shadows of fleeting contentment, and the vast plains of a pain unknown, there, where a small river of regret slowly passes across his field of vision, he cast his seven pebbles and with all his yearning, with a monumental longing for something he hasn't yet experienced, he returned to his beautiful doubt, drained of all certainty.

٤

خذيني إلى بيتٍ بعيدٍ في النسيانِ، بيتٌ كلّما طُرِقَ البابُ يُقالُ الكلامُ ذاتُه، وتُسقَى الزهورُ ذاتُها، ويَبتلُّ غسيلُه بدموعِ جيرانٍ لم يسكنوا جوارَه أبداً. خذيني إلى بيتٍ في الخذلانِ؛ علَّني أشاهدُ صورَ الغائبينَ فلا تذبحني طيلةَ الليلِ رائحةُ البرتقالِ.

٥

عابروكَ كلُّهم..
الجميلونَ، القبيحونَ، الأبرياءُ، الأشرارُ، النساءُ، الفراشاتُ، الأغاني، الأنهُرُ
الأمنياتُ، الموتى كماءٍ يعبرُ سلّةَ قشٍّ.
الماءُ هو الماءُ، والسلّةُ صارت تلمعُ،
تلمعُ صافيةً، كفكرةٍ قديمةٍ مُجرَّبةٍ.

4

Take me to a far-off home in Oblivion, a home that each time there's a knock at the door the same words are uttered, the same flowers watered, the wash drenched in the tears of neighbors who never lived next to it. Take me to a home in Betrayal, maybe I can look at pictures of the missing without getting slaughtered by the smell of oranges
the whole night through.

5

They all pass through you . . .
The beautiful, the ugly, the innocent, the evil, the women,
the butterflies, the songs, the rivers,
the wishes, and the dead like water through a straw basket.
Water is water and now the basket glistens,
it glistens purely like a tried-and-true idea.

٦

كيف يرتكبُ العفوَ قلبي وهو يفكُّ أزرارَ القميصِ؟ هكذا أنوِّمُ قلادةَ البراءةِ تحتَ وسادةِ الاشتهاءِ، أعصرُ داليتَينِ مِنْ ظِلٍّ في فَمِ العطَشِ. لا مَحَلَّ لهُ مِن الصَفحِ وقتي حينَ أذِنْتِ لَهُ بالعبورِ، حينَ لمْ يكنْ الغريبُ يعرفُ أنَّهُ أنَّةٌ في حديثِ الغريبةِ، ومدىً يتفتّحُ في حدسِها لولا أنْ هَمَستْ لنهرِهِ الناهضِ باكتمالِ الهدير.

٧

ليستِ الصدفةُ مَنْ سلّمَتْنا الوديعةَ مثقلةً بالنعاسِ في صباحٍ مُبَكّرٍ، ولا قالبُ السُكّرِ حينَ أذابَتْهُ مياهُ الخطيئةِ بينَ أصابعِنا كانَ صدفةَ الكيمياءِ، ليستْ هي مَن ألقى بالنبوءاتِ بينَ أقدامِنا لنعبرَ حقلَ ألغامٍ وفاكهةٍ، وليست هي مَن عطَّلَ المِصعدَ بُرهةً لنقطفَ قُبلةً من شوكٍ، ولا هي جرَّبتْ حظَّنا، وأغلقتِ البابَ فلمْ يدخلْهُ الهواءُ المُعَتَّقُ بذكرياتٍ وأراجيحَ نبيلةٍ. هي ليستْ إلا صورةً مُعَلَّقةً على حائطٍ لا يراهُ سوايَ تفرُّ منها الطيورُ ويسيلُ دمُ المسافةِ.

6

How does my heart commit the act of pardon while unbuttoning the shirt? This is how I put the necklace of innocence to sleep under the pillow of desire, I squeeze two grape clusters of shadow into the mouth of thirst. My time has no case for reprieve once you've let it pass, when a stranger didn't know he was a moan in another stranger's story, or an expanse opening into her stranger's intuition, had she not whispered to his awakened river that it had reached the fullness of its roar.

7

It wasn't chance that handed us the bundle in trust heavy with sleep one early morning, nor was the sugar cube melting between our fingers with the water of sin a chemical fluke; it didn't hurl prophecies at our feet to pass through mine and fruit fields; it didn't stop the elevator for a bit so we could pick a kiss of thorn, it didn't tempt our fate and shut the door to aged air laden with memories and noble swings — it is nothing but a picture only I can see hanging on a wall, birds flee it, and the blood of distance flows.

٨

كمعبدٍ وثنيٍّ يفقدُ أتباعَه، ينكشفُ اتساعُ القلبِ في الصلَواتِ، لمْ يَعُدْ لبَخُورِ الروحِ والتعاويذِ القديمةِ أنْ تَسترَ عُريَ المكانِ، ولا تمتماتِ الصلواتِ المُرتجَلةِ في نهارِكَ المُتطاولِ أنْ تُسنَدَ ساقَ الإلهِ المبتورةِ، ولا أنْ تُبدِّلَ الرايةَ الباليةَ فوقَ الحائطِ الأخيرِ. أنتَ وحدكَ في الريحِ تماماً، وليسَ في جيبكَ شيءٌ غيرَ أسفٍ صغيرٍ لآخرِ الأصدقاءِ ألقوا بهِ على درجِ التحيةِ كدَينٍ قديم.

٩

وتُغنّي لكَ أمّي ساعةَ جلستِها للحنينِ، ساعةَ تفْتحُ شبّاكَها تلُمُّ خيباتِ الجيرانِ لتقارنَ خيبتَها قَبلَ أنْ تنامَ. تنفضُ عن سجّادةِ الليلِ غُبارَ أحلامِها، وعن سجّادةِ النهارِ غبارَ غيابِكَ، لماذا وأنت تسرقُ أيّامَها كلَّها وتمضي، لايوقِفُكَ الشرطيّ؟! لماذا تُسندُ صورتَكَ المائلةَ وتدعو لكَ أنْ يُباسمَكَ النهارُ، ويُتمَّ وردتَهُ عليكَ إلى أجلٍ غيرِ مُسَمّى، فيما تَميلُ بوصلتُكَ بعيداً عنِ القلبِ، بعيداً عنِ العينِ، بعيداً عن اللهِ؟!

8

Like a pagan temple losing its congregants, the vastness
of the heart is revealed in prayer, the soul's incense and
ancient incantations no longer cover the nakedness of the place,
nor does the muttering of improvised prayer in your long day
hold up the deity's severed leg or replace the tattered banner
on the last wall. You stand in the wind all by yourself, nothing
in your pocket but a bit of regret over the last of the friends
tossed at the steps of greeting like an old debt.

9

My mother sings to you the hour she sits longing, the hour she
opens her window and gathers the failures of the neighbors
comparing them with hers before going to bed. She shakes the
dust of her dreams off the evening rug, and the dust of your
absence off the daytime rug, how is that you steal all her days
and move on, yet no policeman arrests you? Why does she
straighten out your tilted picture and pray for the day to smile
and bestow its garland upon you until who knows when, and
all the while your compass strays from the heart,
from the eye, and from God?

١٠

لقلبكَ رائحةٌ تدلُّ وردَ الحديقةِ على خُطاكَ، فتفيضُ أحزانُها وجعاً له صوتُ ناي يتبعُكَ أنَّى مشَيتَ. أعرفُ الآنَ لماذا توغلُ في صحرائِكَ مُتبتِّلًا، ساهماً ووحيداً كنايٍ منسيٍ في خزانةِ قديمة.

١١

ليسَ لي كمنجةٌ لأسكبَ روحي مرةً واحدةً على الرملِ، ولا شيءَ يرشَحُ مِن مسائي غيرَ صوتِ عبدِ الحليمِ وأبي ذرٍّ يتسامران تحتَ أزيزِ جنادبِ الجيرانِ ونيرانِ كتبي الصديقةِ. آنَ أنْ تَكفَّ الضغينةُ عن غوايتِها إذنْ، وأنْ تَكتبَ الملائكةُ سِيرةَ الخطّائينَ مِثلي بشكلٍ أجملَ، وأخيراً آنَ أنْ يخسرَ أبي رهانَهُ الصغيرَ علَيَّ.

10

Your heart has a scent that leads garden roses to your steps, then sadness overflows with an ache that sounds like a flute following you wherever you go. Now I know why you wade into your desert having taken the vows, absent-minded and lonesome like a forgotten flute in an old closet.

11

I don't have a violin to spill my soul all at once on the sand, and nothing seeps from my evening except the voice of Abdel Halim and Companion Abu Dharr sitting together by the chirping sound of the neighbors' crickets and the friendly fire of my books. It's time then for resentment to cease its temptation, and for the angels to write the life of sinners like mine more beautifully, and for my father, finally, to lose the small wager he put on me.

١٢

الراقصُ بينَ سيِّدَتَينِ في حُمَّى دبكةٍ عارمةٍ، مكتظّاً بعطرِ «خوليو إجليسياس»، وشهوةِ «الحمامِ بالفريك»، الراقصُ بينَ سيدتينِ يشربُ «الكوكتيلَ» جُرعةً واحدةً، ويلكُنُ كلّما ردَّ التحيّةَ — بفرنسيّةٍ ناعمةٍ — على جارِهِ المُلتحِي. يعرفُ أنّ شفتَينِ تعضّانِ قَلبَهُ حمامتانِ تلمّان عالياً عُشَّ نَزَقِه المتناثرِ جُرأةً ورغباتٍ، أنَّ يَداً واحدةً لضميرِه تصفعُهُ بقوةٍ، حينَ ينامُ في الغرفةِ الرماديّةِ ويفاخذُ وحدتَهُ، على وقعِ ظِلٍّ شفيفٍ يصفّقُ له.

١٣

كُن قاضياً بينَ شجرِ الجانبينِ، يختصمونَ أيُّهم يسرقُ نَظرتَكَ الساهمةَ ويفضُّ بكارةَ يومِكَ. كُن رَجلَ الجُمُعَةِ المُملَّ وأَقمْ صلاةً سريعةً ولا تعُدْ للبيتِ قبلَ أن يحملَكَ البرتقالُ وتغبطَكَ المئذنةُ. كن «توم هانكس» وقُل: يا اللّهُ! كلُّ شيءٍ على ما يرامُ يا أولادُ. كُنْ أيَّ شيءٍ، فقط رُدَّ السلامَ على موتِكَ الجميلِ في المِرآةِ.

12

The dancer between two ladies in the fever pitch of a *dabke*,
overflowing with the scent of *Julio Iglesias* and the desire for
a dish of pigeon with *freekeh*, the dancer between two ladies
chugs a cocktail in one gulp, and garbles — in soft French —
each time he returns his bearded neighbor's greetings. He knows
the two lips biting at his heart are two doves gathering high
the nest of his mischief strewn about with boldness and desire,
and that the single hand of his conscience slaps him hard
as he sleeps alone in the gray room rubbing himself against his
solitude, to the tune of a translucent shadow applauding him.

13

Be a judge between the trees of both sides, battling who will
grab your wandering gaze and deflower your day. Be boring
Man Friday and make a quick prayer, don't go back home
until you're carried by oranges and envied by a minaret.
Be Tom Hanks and say: God! Everything is great, guys. Be
anything, just wave back to your beautiful death in the mirror.

١٤

ربّما كنتَ تهذي حينَ قلتَ لها أنّ مِرآةً واحدةً لا تكفي لوسامةِ يومِكِ البهيِّ، وأنّ شارعاً سيفرحُ كثيراً لغبارِ مشاويرَ فكّرتِ بها طوالَ الليلِ، أنّ شرفةً تُمنّي الهواءَ بعبوركِ المُنتظرِ هي شرفةٌ مُتيَّمةٌ بكِ إلى حدِّ الجنونِ. ربّما كنتَ تَهذي حين قلتَ لها أنّ كلَّ كفٍّ لمْ تُصافِحْكِ هي صَحراءُ مؤجَّلةٌ، وكلَّ مِرآة ابتسمْتِ لها أيقونةٌ للعذابِ، لكنّكَ كنتَ في كاملِ الصحوِ حينَ لمْ تَقُلْ لها بعدَ كلِّ هذا : أحبُّكِ.

١٥

كلّما مشيتُ أكثرَ في طرقاتِ اللغةِ تمنيتُ لو عُدتُ حيثُ بدأتُ، وكلّما تهيّأتُ لصيدِ خاطرةٍ ما تقودُني اللغةُ مرةً تلو مرةٍ إلى سراديبِها الموحشةِ؛ فمتى أخرُجُ مِنْ متاهتي وأعرفُ أنّ هناكَ شيئاً يستحِقُّ أنْ نعيشَهُ خارجَ تلكَ الغوايةِ؟

14

Maybe you were delirious when you told her that a single mirror is not enough for the beauty of her glorious day, and that the street will delight in the dust of promenades you thought about all night, that a balcony teasing the air by her anticipated passing is a balcony infatuated with her to the point of madness. Maybe you were delirious when you told her every hand that didn't shake hers is a desert deferred and every mirror she smiled at is an icon of torment, but you were fully lucid and didn't tell her, after all this: I love you.

15

The more I walk in the pathways of language, the more I wish I'd go back to where I started, every time I ready myself to hunt down a thought, language leads me time and again to its haunting vaults; when will I get out of my labyrinth and fathom that there is something worth doing outside of this lure?

١٦

أعرفُ أنّني كلّما غادرتُ البيتَ عادتِ الأشياءُ إلى طبيعتِها: فتاتُ الأسئلةِ يتسلّقُ الحائطَ، المكتبةُ تسبحُ في المائدةِ، والبابُ ينادي على الجيرانِ كي يتقاسموا غِيابي، بَيْدَ أنّ شيئاً واحداً غامضاً لا أفهمُهُ: كيفَ تَظَلُّ الموسيقى كما هي: موسيقى وحسب!

١٧

إلى السوسناتِ اللواتي غَفَونَ جِوارَ دارٍ عتيقةٍ، إلى الحَصَى يدورُ حولَ ناصيةِ البيتِ مطروداً من الرحمةِ، عارياً من الأملِ، إلى الكلماتِ الرخيصةِ نبذُرُها على الجيرانِ وأغنياتِ السابعةِ صباحاً، إلى غطائي الثقيلِ ينامُ جِواري كما يفعلُ الحُبُّ في الشتاءِ وأنا أتذكّرُ شمسَكِ الغائبةَ، إلى حُزني الذي يكتبُ وأصابعي التي تلُوكُ الولاءَ، ليس لديَّ ما أقولُهُ لكم.

١٨

أراكَ الأغاني في عينِ أمّي بين كفّيها تلُمُّ بقايا المساءِ، وكانَ شتاء. أراكَ جوقةً تائهةً تعزفُ لحنَ غيابِكَ، فيَسْتَدفِئُ القلبُ نارَ الكمنجةَ، ويُدرِكُ ماذا أضاع. أراكَ الطيورَ التي لا تملُّ الوقوفَ أمامي، والمسافاتُ تنقرُ الروحَ وتقطَعُ منّي الذراع.

16

I know every time I leave the house everything reverts to its nature: crumbs of questions climb the walls, the library swims in the table, and the door calls out to the neighbors to divvy up my absence; but there's one thing I don't understand: how does music stay itself: simply music.

17

To the irises dozing by an old abode, to the pebbles circled around the entrance to the house banished from mercy and devoid of hope, to the cheap words we spent on the neighbors and seven-in-the morning songs, to my heavy blanket sleeping next to me as love in winter while I remember your absent sun. To my sadness that writes and to my fingers mumbling fealty, I have nothing to say to you.

18

You're songs I see in my mother's eye gathering between her palms the remains of the evening, and it was winter. You're a lost ensemble I see playing the tune of your absence, the heart drawing the violin's flame and realizing what it had lost. You're birds I see never tiring to stand before me, like distances that peck the soul and rip my arm off.

١٩

ستكونُ أصابعُكَ ثمارَ برتقالٍ، وساعِدُكَ ساريةً لعلَمٍ مُنتصِرٍ، وقلبُكَ محطةَ قطارٍ أخيرةٍ،
حينها لنْ تكونَ هنا؛ بلْ في مكانٍ يصعُبُ وصفُهُ، تشرحُ للملائكةِ المُنبهرينَ كيف أمكنَ للحُبِّ أن يصنعَ المُعجزةَ.

٢٠

أعرفُ أنّكِ تتمايلينَ بغناءِ حالمٍ كلّما مرَّ جوارَكِ عُشّاقٌ أو مسّوا حنينَكِ القديمَ،
أنّ قشعريرةً كامنةً تسري فيكِ من أعمقِ جذرٍ كرعشةِ أنثى حتى آخرِ ورقةِ «كينا» في آخرِ غصنٍ قريبٍ مِن الغيمِ، لكنّي لا أعرفُ ماذا أصِفُ وجعَكِ حين يحفرون قلباً عليكِ، ويمضون تاركينَ ذكرى زارعِكِ الغائبِ منتصبةً أمامَكِ غابةً يَلفُّها الحريقُ.

٢١

رصاصةُ الأبِ صمتٌ،
رصاصةُ الأمِّ دمعةٌ،
رصاصةُ العاشقِ وردةٌ،
رصاصةُ الأرضِ قبرٌ،
رصاصةُ اللّهِ كلمةٌ.

19

Your fingers will be the fruit of orange trees, your arm the staff
for a victorious flag, and your heart the train's last station,
you won't be here then but somewhere hard to describe,
explaining to bedazzled angels how love can accomplish
a miracle.

20

I know you sway in dreamy song every time lovers pass you
by or touch your old longing, that a shiver runs through
you from the deepest root like a woman's tremor to the last
eucalyptus leaf on the last branch closest to the cloud, but
I don't know how to describe your pain when they engrave
a heart on you, leaving the memory of your absent sower
standing before you like a forest engulfed by fire.

21

The bullet of the father is silence,
the bullet of the mother a tear,
the bullet of the lover a rose,
the bullet of Earth a grave,
the bullet of God a word.

٢٢

منذورةٌ للجنونِ، لهاويةٍ ملونةٍ، خيولُ روحِنا، لانعتاقِها الأبديِّ من أجسامِنا، من رفقةِ الأرضِ التي مشينا عليها طويلاً. الآن نعرفُ كيف ترَفرفُ الغيمةُ حدَّ البكاءِ، كيف تُخرِجُ الوسامةُ مِن جَيبِ ساحرِ الصباحِ مناديلَ وفراشاتٍ، تُنبتُ الصحراءُ غاباتَها الوارِفةَ، تمطرُ السماءُ بالوناتٍ ويصدحُ الرعاةُ بأسرارِنا القديمةِ.

٢٣

لِمَنْ تَدُقُّ أجراسُ روحي؟!
لغبارِ نافذةٍ يتوافدُ عليها الكلامُ ذاتُه كلَّ يومٍ؟
لغيمةٍ نائمةٍ على رصيفِ الكتابةِ منذُ عامينِ، ثلاثةٍ، ولمْ يعبره أحدٌ؟
لبريدِ دوائرِ بحيرةٍ أَلْقَيْتُ فيها أحجارَ قلبي ولمْ تزلْ نائمةً؟
لطابورِ خبزٍ تصطفُّ عليه أحلامُنا المُتَّسِخَةُ، فيطولُ جوعُها وانتظارُنا؟
لِمَنْ تَدُقُّ أجراسُ روحي؟ لِمَنْ؟

22

The horses of our soul — in their eternal emancipation from our bodies, out of the kinship of a land we have long walked on — are ordained to madness, to a colorful abyss. Now we know how the cloud flutters to the edge of tears, how charm brings kerchiefs and butterflies out of a magician's pocket, how the desert grows its lush forests, how the sky rains balloons and shepherds sing out our old secrets.

23

For whom do the bells of my soul toll?
For the dust of a window visited by the same words every day?
For a cloud sleeping on the sidewalk of writing for two,
three years, and no one has crossed it?
For the script of the ripples in a lake where I tossed
the stones of my heart, and that still sleeps?
For a breadline where our grimy dreams line up,
prolonging their hunger and our wait?
For whom do the bells of my soul toll? For whom?

٢٤

أجِدُني في ثَنيَّاتِ الوداعِ،
في سياقِ السؤالِ عن القافلةِ حيثُ تركَتْني خلفَها القصيدةُ،
أجدُني في رمالِ الأبجديَّةِ الناعمةِ غارقاً فيكِ،
في جموعِ الهُتافِ الصّموتِ نكايةً في ثرثرةِ أغانٍ، حين لا يُومِئُ قلبي
نحو خِبائكِ،
أجِدُني مِثلَ أنبياءَ في عاديّاتِهم حين لا يُتلَى عليَّ شيءٌ من كتابِ اللقاءِ

٢٥

يا حنينُ: لا تقِفْ هكذا خجِلاً أمامَ العتبةِ، أنتَ لمْ تغِبْ أبداً، ولمْ تَكُن ضيفاً سريعَ الزيارةِ. أيّها الوارِفُ مثلَ عريشةِ عنبٍ تأكلُ الهواءَ كلّما تنفَّسْنا، وتشربُ الندى والحكاياتِ والكلماتِ المنسيَّةَ بعدَ خروجِ المساءِ. هُنا يا حنينُ، هُنا جَلستُكَ الهادئةُ جِواري، نُقلِّبُ في دفترٍ لشجرِ العائلةِ، وصورٍ لطيورِ القلبِ حين تَحُطُّ لتنقرَ صمتي.

24

I find myself on the high road of Farewell,
moving to ask about the caravan at the place where the poem left
me behind, I find myself in the soft sand of the alphabet
sinking in you, in a silent throng clamoring to spite the chatter
of song, when my heart nods not toward your dwelling,
I find myself like hackneyed prophets, when nothing
from the Book of Encounter speaks to me.

25

O longing, don't stand like that, shy at the threshold,
you never left, nor were you a fleeting guest. You're as luscious
as a grapevine eating the air each time we breathe, drinking
dew, stories, and words forgotten after evening breaks, here,
O longing, here your quiet sits with me, leafing through
the book of a family tree, and pictures of birds of
the heart as they land to peck at my silence.

٢٦

سفرٌ يركضُ والساعةُ واقفةٌ،
نهرٌ يَجمعُ أغراضَهُ في جيبي المثقوبِ،
ليلٌ يعلكُ نهاراتي ويغادرُ والساعةُ واقفةٌ.
مدنٌ تشهقُ باروداً وتثاؤباً، تحلُمُ بطيورٍ مِن نَرجِسٍ، والساعةُ . . . ،
لا عَلَمَ يرفرفُ لي،
لا طيرَ يحطُّ على النافذةِ،
وأنا ساعةُ حائطٍ واقفةٌ تعلنُ الواحدةَ.

٢٧

لخروجِها من سِجْنِها يصفِّقُ التاريخُ للأمكنةِ، لانعتاقِها من أُحبولةِ الدائرةِ، من دورةِ الموتِ والحياةِ، من دورةِ «الألكترونِ» حولَ ذرَّةٍ يابسةٍ، من دورةِ الأرضِ حولَ شمسِها القائظةِ، من دورةِ الماءِ والطينِ والمصائرِ المريرةِ المتشابهةِ، يصفِّقُ التاريخُ للأمكنةِ.

26

Travel runs and the clock stands still, a river gathers its things in my torn pocket, night gnaws at my days and moves on, and the clock stands still.
Cities exhale gunpowder and yawn, dreaming of birds made of narcissus, and the clock . . . , no flag flies for me, no bird lands at my window, and I'm an idle clock, reading 1:00.

27

For having left their prison, history applauds places, for their emancipation from the noose of the circle, from the cycle of death and life, from the revolution of the electron around its hard nucleus, from the turning of the earth around its burning sun, from the cycle of water and mud, and from bitter fates like to like, history applauds places.

٢٨

الغزالُ الواقفُ مبهوراً بالصمتِ في لوحةِ الحائطِ، يهبطُ كلَّ ليلةٍ، يَرعى العشبَ في حُلْمي، ويشربُ من راحتيَّ دموعِي، ويحملُ التنهّداتِ إلى بيتِها البعيدِ في التلالِ البعيدةِ. لم يكنْ شيئاً غريباً أنْ يرتَبِكَ هذا المشهدُ، فأنامُ في حُلمِهِ كعشبةٍ على كتِفِ الحديقةِ، كتَعَبٍ في حُضْنِ اللّيلِ، وأنْ يَمُرَّ الغزالُ جواري — حين أذكرُ اسمَها — مبهوراً بالغناءِ ومختالاً بجرأةِ المفارقةِ.

28

The gazelle standing still dazzled by the silence in the painting on the wall, comes down every night to graze on the grass in my dream, drink tears from my palms, and carry sighs to their faraway home in the distant hills. It wasn't strange for that scene to go awry and for me to sleep in its dream like a blade of grass on the shoulder of the garden, like exhaustion in the embrace of night, and for the gazelle to pass me by — when I call her name — dazzled by the song and prancing to the boldness of the paradox.

٢٩

ما لَمْ أقُلْهُ لي مَرَّةً ومشيث، صارَ همساً يُحاذي وقعَ أقدامي، يسرقُ من أصابعِ فكرتي خواتمَ صمتِها، يلاحقُها كعاشقٍ في البساتينِ والمرايا، يراودُ شيطانَها في الصّعودِ المتأخِّرِ ليلاً على درجِ المتاهةِ حيثُ الغيومُ والقصائدُ والنساءُ والحروبُ تغزلُ كنزةً ناعمةً تدفِّيءُ ليليَ الطويلَ الأناةِ.
ما لَمْ أقُلْهُ لي مَرَّةً وبكيث، صارَ نواحاً يصارعُ روحي في السماواتِ، حيثُ وحيُ الأبجديّةِ ينزلُ من غيمٍ قريبٍ. يعجنُها بدمِ الأخرين في طاحونةِ انشغالِي، وليسَ يتركُها تُبَلِّلُ ارتباكاً و قُبَلاً عندَ شرفةِ امرأةٍ من صلاةٍ.
ما لَمْ أقُلْهُ لي لا يحتملُ السكوتَ، فخاً كبيراً كبيراً تصيرُ الحياةُ.

٣٠

موسيقى مضيئةٌ تسيلُ من زوايا الوقتِ، مِنَ اللوحةِ الناعسةِ، مِنَ الأكوابِ الملوَّنةِ، من أيدينا التائهةِ في عناقِها المباغِتِ،
تسيلُ من سقفِ الغرفةِ مطراً أزرقَ يبلِّلُ ثيابَنا بأغانٍ لا تنتهي، فهل يشبهُكَ الحبُّ يا اللّهُ؟
الحبُّ الذي يتكلمُ الجميعُ عنه، ولمْ يرَه احدٌ؟

29

What I did not say to me once and walked on became
whispers dogging my footsteps, stealing
from the fingers of my idea rings of their silence, pursuing
them like a lover in gardens and mirrors, tempting its demons
in the late night ascent up the stairs of the labyrinth where
clouds, poems, women, and wars knit a soft sweater
that warms my long forbearing night.
What I did not say to me once and cried, became wails
wrestling with my soul in the heavens, where the revelation
of the alphabet descends from a nearby cloud, kneading
my soul with the blood of others in the mill of my disquiet,
not letting it and the wails moisten the confusion and kisses
at the balcony of a woman made of prayer. What I did not say
to me cannot bear being left unspoken,
turning life into one huge snare.

30

Luminous music flows from the corners of time, from the
sleepy painting, from the colored cups, from our arms lost in
its sudden embrace, it flows from the ceiling of the room like
blue rain drenching our clothes in endless song, does love look
like you, O God? The love everyone talks about,
but no one has ever seen?

٣١

زِحامٌ على النافذةِ،
قطيعٌ مِنَ المفرداتِ يطرقُ بابي، وأنا أخَبِّئُ رأسي تحتَ
وسادةٍ من فراغٍ.
أريدُ البراءةَ من كلِّ سطرٍ كتبْتُهُ، أريدُ البكاءَ على كلِّ يدٍ صافحَتْ كِتاباً.
زِحامٌ على النافذةِ، قطيعٌ من المفرداتِ، وقلبي باردٌ يطرُقُهُ حديدُ
الدهشةِ.

٣٢

نهرٌ ووصايا لمْ يرتكِبْها، والنبوءاتُ قالتْ لهُ كلَّ يومٍ: تصيرُ سحاباً.
سطرٌ ومرايا لم يقترفْها، والخساراتُ قالتْ له كلَّ حُلْمٍ: تصيرُ هُراءً.
حجرٌ ومياهٌ لم ينتظرْها، والشهواتُ قالتْ لهُ كلَّ عُمْرٍ: تصيرُ تراباً.
حجرُ نردٍ يضحكُ، حجرُ نردٍ يحزَنُ، كلَّ يومٍ، ولا يكترثُ لحديثِ الحياةِ.

31

A throng at the window, a flock of vocabularies knocks at my
door, and I hide my head under a pillow of emptiness.
I want to disown every line I wrote, I want to cry over every
hand that has welcomed a book. A throng at the window,
a flock of vocabularies, my heart is cold, hammered
by the iron of bedazzlement.

32

A river and commandments it doesn't carry out, and
prophesies tell it daily: you'll be cloud. A line and mirrors
it doesn't commit, losses tell it in every dream: you'll be utter
drivel. Stone and water it doesn't expect, desires tell it in every
life: you'll be dust. Every day dice roll high, dice roll low,
and pay no mind to the chatter of life.

٣٣

القبائلُ المهاجرةُ مِنْ بينِ أصابعِكِ بشَّرَتْ بانتصارِ الحضارةِ، التَماثيلُ المُقلَّدَةُ عنكِ في بلادٍ تعبدُ الفرحَ، زاولَتْ مهنتَها بفرحٍ كبيرٍ أيضاً، الأنهرُ الحالمةُ أنْ تصيرَ مظلّةً لمرورِكِ، تحايلَتْ على الوقت، وصارتْ أنهُراً سعيدةً مرسومةً على ثيابِكِ، انا كنتُ أَمكَرَهم جميعاً حينَ صرتُ قاطعَ طريقٍ، والغجريَّ المتوحِّشَ قاتلَ فكرتي المجنونةِ عنكِ.

٣٤

يا عصفورَ قلبي، تعالَ انقرْ خَدّي؛ ليُمطرَ اثنا عشرَ مَوسِماً مِنَ الغناءِ على شُبّاكِ روحي. هكذا قالتِ الأمُّ لصغيرها قبلَ أن يصدِّقَها ويصيرَ لهُ أذرعٌ من ريشٍ، قَبلَ أنْ يُصبحَ وَجْهُها لوحةً مسافرةً، والشُّبّاكُ إطارَها المُقيمَ.

33

Tribes migrating between your fingers proclaim the triumph
of civilization, the statues, replicas of you, in a country
worshipping joy, also pursue their jobs joyfully, rivers
dreaming to be umbrellas trick time as you pass and
become happy rivers painted on your clothes, I was the most
cunning of all when I became a highway bandit and
the wild gypsy killing my own crazy idea of you.

34

O you, bird of my heart, come and peck at my cheeks to rain
down twelve seasons of song on the window of my soul. This
is what a mother told her little one before he believed her and
grew feathered limbs, before her face turned into a transient
painting and the window its resident frame.

٣٥

مرةً كُنْ برتقالياً أيُّها البحرُ، ويا سماءُ أَمطري مرةً باتّجاهكِ، فيطيرَ الأطفالُ نحوَ الغيمِ، وتنتحبَ المدرسةُ، فاجِئيني يا حبيبتي أنّ دجاجاتِنا لها أجنحةٌ مِنْ ورقِ العُملاتِ، أنّ الشارعَ خرجَ عَنْ وَقارِه، وصارَ قوسَ قُزحَ يُدخِّنُ أغنياتٍ. يا أولادُ، جَرِّبوا — حينَ أنامُ — عالياً ضحكةَ البطّيخِ، لأصحو مِنَ الكابوسِ، وأعرِفَ انّني لم أَكُنْ جِداراً يُعَلِّقُ المارُّونَ عليهِ ايّامَهمُ الباليةَ.

٣٦

هل أتاكِ في عُريِهِ الليليِّ قَلبي جَواداً لمْ تصادفْهُ رحمةُ الرصاصِ، ولا صادَفَتْهُ في آخِرِ الحربِ قبلةُ الحياةِ؟ هل اتاكِ لا يشبهُني؟ يسيلُ مِنْ فَمِهِ عسلُ الناياتِ، كما الغيمِ لا يشبهُ المطرَ، ولا تُشبهُ الموسيقى شجنَ الوتَرِ. هل اتاكِ يُقشِّرُ حُزنَ المُغنِّي عنْ قمرِ الحكايةِ، ويَعصرُ جدائلَ النّهرِ مِنْ سَهَرِ الانتظارِ؟ جَواداً يحملُ فارسَهُ مَيّتاً ويَمشي، إنّه قلبي يدقُّ بابَ غيابِكِ عارياً كنصفِ تُفّاحةٍ، وفارغاً مثلَ يومٍ باهتٍ بعدَ حربٍ طويلةٍ.

35

For once, just be orange, O sea, and you, heaven, rain just
once in your own direction, so kids fly toward the clouds,
and school weeps. Surprise me, O love of mine, so our
chickens have wings of paper money, and the street loses
its sobriety to become a rainbow smoking songs.
O Kids, do your best — when I'm asleep — to laugh as loud as
watermelon, to wake me up from the nightmare, and realize
I'm not a wall where passersby hang their worn-out days.

36

Did my heart ever come to you in its nightly nakedness like a
steed that never ran into the mercy of bullets, or the kiss of life
at the end of the war? Did it come not looking like me?
Its mouth dripping with the honey of flutes, like clouds
that don't look like rain, or music like the sorrow of the string?
Did it come to you peeling the singer's sadness off the moon of
the story, and wringing the braids of the river from the long
night's wait? A steed carrying his dead knight canters on, my
heart knocking at the door of your absence naked as half
an apple and empty as a lackluster day after long war.

٣٧

هَبْ أنّكَ بُستانيٌّ تَبْذُرُ حقلَكَ بالموسيقى؛ فيصير العشبُ على أطرافِ أصابعِكَ نقوشَ الحنّاءِ، ويفيضُ الماءُ. يزهرُ خزفٌ من صَلصالٍ مَشغولٍ بدموعِ الوردِ العاشقِ، ويفيضُ الماءُ، يَنبتُ مَرجٌ فوقَ المرجِ، وسماءٌ فوقَ سماءٍ، وقوسُ كمنجةِ روحِكَ يتصيّدُ كلَّ طيورِ الزَّهوِ. تصطفُّ أوانٍ من عطرِ الحبِّ على خَطِّ ظِلالِكَ في حقلٍ مجنون. انتَ الآنَ قَطفتَ مِنَ الجنّةِ قبضةَ ريحٍ، صِرتَ نبيَّ اللحظةِ، والمُتَصوِّف، المَمْسوسَ، العرَّافَ، السائرَ فوقَ الماءِ.

٣٨

النبيذُ لمْ يأتِ بعد والشجرةُ التي اظلّتني طِوالَ النهارِ غادرت لتنامَ. وأما صلاتي فوحدُها في العراء، تفتِّشُ عن بابِ اللّه مثلَ نملةٍ في صحنِ عسلٍ كبيرٍ. انا لا اجيدُ الحديثَ إليَّ. انا محضُ ماءٍ عَطِشٌ لماء. والنبيذُ الصمتُ، النبيذُ الكلامُ الذي يجيءُ لينتشيَ مِن دمي لمْ يأتِ بعد.

37

Suppose you're a gardener sowing your field with music, so grass at your fingertips becomes inscriptions in henna, and the water flows. Earthenware blooms out of clay worked with tears of roses in love, and the water brims over, a prairie grows over prairies, a sky over sky, your soul the bow of a violin hunting all the birds of conceit. The bottles of the perfume of love line up along shadow in an infatuated field. Now you've picked from paradise a handful of wind, you've become the prophet of the moment, the mystic, the touched, the soothsayer, the one walking on water.

38

Wine hasn't yet come, the tree shading me all day went to sleep. As for my prayer, it's all alone out in the open looking for the Gate of God like an ant in a big plate of honey. I'm not good at talking to me. I'm merely water thirsty for water. The silence wine, the speech wine, coming to get intoxicated with my blood, isn't yet here.

موسيقى خلفية للحياة

١

أيّار يدقُّ الأبوابَ، يدقُّ الأبوابَ.
يسّاقط مَلَلٌ كثيفٌ من سقوفِ البيوت،
والنباتاتُ قططٌ جرباءَ تحكُّ ظُهورَها بالجدارِ،
تذوي الشبابيكُ الحُبْلى بالكلامِ في ساعةِ الولادةِ، فتَذبُلُ رَغبتي.
وحدُها شَمسُ أيار تروحُ وتَجيء،
ولا أحدَ يتأبّطُ واحةً منسيةً هناكَ في صحراءِ قلبي،
لا أحدَ يحملُ مِظلّةً ويرافقُ الياسمينَ في مرورِه المحتملِ،
لا أحدَ يسألُ الصبّار لماذا يطيلُ صَمتَهُ.
أيّار مازالَ يدُقُّ الأبوابَ ولا أحدَ هُنا يهُمُّه الأمرُ.
الصالةُ المكومةُ طوالَ الوقتِ جوارَ السنواتِ الطيبةِ ماتتْ دونَ أن ننتَبه،
البراءات المنسيّة بينَ صفحاتِ كتابِ الشكِّ والذي لم نقرأهُ إلا في نومِنا
سقطتْ سهواً،
الموتى الذينَ يهتِفُون طِوال المشاجرةِ بيني وبينَ الحياةِ تركوني وحيداً
الأشجارُ التي تسلّقَها الجيرانُ لجمعِ الأخبارِ الرديئة أمطرتْ عصافيرَ
على شكلِ جيرانٍ آخرين،
البيوتُ المسكونةُ بالأشباحِ تمدُّ ألسِنَتَها لعابرِي ذِكرياتي في الظهيرةِ
فيشعرونَ بطمأنينةِ السَّروِ،
لا شيءَ إذاً يستحقُّ البكاءَ، لا شيءَ إذاً يستحقُّ الفرحَ.
ربما لو نكسرُ إشارةَ مرورٍ واحدةٍ؛ واحدةٍ فقط مِن أجلِ هذا الشِّعر المَلول،
من أجلِ الشرطيّ الذي يقودُ بنا سيارةَ الموتى لمُجرَّدِ هدرِ الوقتِ.

BACKGROUND MUSIC FOR LIFE

1

May is knocking on doors, knocking on doors, thick boredom
rolls off the roofs, and the plants are scabby cats scratching
their backs against the wall, windows pregnant with words
fade at the hour of labor — my desire withers. Only the May sun
comes and goes, no one carries a forgotten oasis under their arm
in the desert of my heart. No one holds an umbrella for the
passing jasmine, no one asks why the cactus keeps silent.
May still knocks on the doors and no one cares.
The cluttered living room piled up next to the good years died
without anyone noticing. The innocence forgotten in the pages
of the Book of Doubt, that we read only in our sleep,
fell from neglect, the dead who cheer throughout my quarrel
with life leave me alone, the trees the neighbors climbed
fishing for bad news rained birds in the form of new
neighbors, at noon haunted houses stick their tongues out at
those passing through my memory, and feel the contentment
of cypresses, nothing to cry over then, nothing merits joy.
Maybe if we were to break just one traffic sign,
just one for the sake of this listless poetry, for the sake of a
policeman taking us for a ride
in a hearse just to kill time.

٢

ربما الموتُ يأتي كحلوى بعد حياةٍ كهذه؛ فها أنت ضَجِرُ الفصولِ، فراغٌ يتمدَّدُ في صحراءِ سريرِك، وتحتَ الوسادةِ مِسْخٌ ينامُ كسولاً: كتابُ أعمالِك الكاملة.

لذا أنت تشبهُ «كافكا»، وتغبِطُ الميتينَ كثيراً. ألقِ الحكايةَ من النافذةِ وخبّيء في جيبِكَ تفاصيلَ الرواة، مزقَ الثيابِ، غبارَ الأحذيةِ، دمَ المعركة. الحكايةُ خشبُ الكمان، واللغةُ موسيقى لجناز الحياة.

ها أنا أكتبُ عن الموتِ حينَ أقشِّرُ بصلاً، وعنِ الجنسِ وأنا أرمّمُ الحديقة، ويا ويلي حينَ أكتبُ شِعراً وأنظرُ إلى وجهِها جميل.

2

Maybe death will be a piece of cake after a life like this;
and there you are bored as the seasons, a void extending
in the desert of your bed, and underneath your pillow a lazy
monster sleeps: The book of your *Complete Works*.
That's why you're like Kafka, and you envy the dead.
Throw the story out the window, and keep the narrator's
details in your pocket: shred of clothes, dust of shoes,
and blood of battle. The story is the wood of the violin,
and language is the funeral music for life.
Here I am writing about death while peeling onions,
and about sex while I revamp the garden. What, oh what
will become of me when I write poetry
and look at her beautiful face.

٣

حذاءٌ بُنّيٌّ بنقوشٍ على المقدمةِ ورقبةٍ قصيرةٍ يتسكّعُ في بيتٍ مهجورٍ؛ بينَ غرفِ النومِ وخزانةِ الصحون، بينَ الأسرّةِ المتربة وكراسي الطاولةِ الكبيرةِ، يمُدُّ رَقْبَتَه قليلاً ويمشي، لا يفقدُ الأملَ، لا يشكو الوحدةَ، ولا يتذمّر، يمشي ساعةً كلّ يومٍ لا أكثر تماماً كما أوصى طبيبُ السكّري، الوصايا التي لم ينتبِه لها أحد؛ سِوى حذاءٌ بنيٌّ مُتعبٌ بنقوشٍ على المقدمةِ يُحدِثُ صريراً خافتاً كلّ يومٍ في قيلولةِ جيراني.

٤

تقول الحكايةُ أنّ شجرةَ «كينا» صارتْ قارباً حينَ اشتهت البحرَ، وأنّي لو لم أكفْ عن اشتهائِك فربما أصيرُ شجرةَ «كينا». لا بأسَ إذن، فهناك متّسع في الطريقِ لشجرةٍ أخرى ما دُمْتِ ستمرّين مِن أمامي كلّ صباحٍ مِثلما كانَ يحدثُ قبلَ أن تسْرَقَني مِنكَ الحكايةُ.

3

A brown wing tip shoe with a low-cut collar loiters
about in an abandoned home; between the bedrooms and
the china cabinet, between the dusty beds and the chairs
at the big table, it stretches its collar a little and walks,
doesn't lose hope, doesn't feel lonely, doesn't complain,
and walks an hour a day and no more just like the diabetes
doctor ordered — advice no one listens to, except for
the brown wing tip shoe that squeaks softly
everyday while my neighbors nap.

4

As the story goes, the eucalyptus tree became a canoe when
it desired the sea, and I, if I don't stop wanting you, perhaps
I'll turn into a eucalyptus tree. Alright then, there's room on
the road for another tree as long as you'll pass by me every
morning as it was before the story stole me from you.

٥

أتوقُ إلى آلةٍ موسيقى تعزِفُ لحناً غيرَ تلكَ الحروفِ، ليسَ لها صوتٌ يتكسَّر مثلَ قشرِ البيضِ، ليسَ لها رائحةُ تلامذةٍ يرسبونَ من الذاكرةِ. آلةُ موسيقى تبلِّلُ مستَمِعيها فيخرجونَ من النصّ غَرقى. آلةٌ تبدأُني بالسلام، أصفِّفُ أمامها ارتباكي طوالَ المساء، ألقي بها على شاشةِ الفجرِ كصحنٍ فارغٍ من الدهشةِ. كمنجةٌ من خشبِ الصمتِ، نايٌ مِن حريرِ الدموعِ، امرأةٌ تسيلُ عليَّ كمطرٍ على نافذة.

٦

النادلُ يمسحُ طاولتي، ولا يغادرُ.
قلتُ: أريدُ صديقاً واحداً يكسرُ صَمتي ولا يطير، أريدُ نافذةً للزّفيرِ المعتَّقِ في جيوبي، وسجائرَ.
والنادلُ يمسحُ طاولتي، ولا يغادرُ.
أريدُ هواءً يجلسُ معي، وبلاداً بِلا ذكريات، وكلاماً يسيلُ من قلبي سِربُ نملٍ طويلٍ، طويلٍ.
والنادلُ يمسحُ طاولتي ولا يغادرُ.
أريدُ وِحدَتي كاملةً، غصَّتي كاملةً، أمزِّقُها على مَهلٍ فتضحكَ لي صورُ الغائبينَ.
يجلسُ النادلُ معي، والموتُ يمسحُ الطاولةَ ولا يغادرُ.

5

I long for a musical instrument that plays a tune other than
these keys, without a sound that breaks like eggshells, without
the scent of students dropping out of memory. A musical
instrument that whets its listeners leaving them drowned by
the score. This instrument greets me first, I set my nerves
up in front of it all evening, then toss it out on the screen
of dawn aghast, like an empty plate. A violin of the wood
of silence, a reed pipe from the silk of tears, a woman
flowing over me like rain on a windowpane.

6

The waiter clears my table, and won't leave.
I said: I want one friend to break my silence — and not
fly — I want a way out for the vintage breath in my pocket,
and cigarettes.
The waiter clears my table, and won't leave.
I'd like air to sit with and a country without memories,
and words flowing from my heart
like a long, long troop of ants.
The waiter clears my table, and won't leave.
I want my solitude with everything on it, my choke well done,
I tear them slowly so the pictures of the missing laugh.
The waiter sits with me, death clears the table and won't leave.

٧

لماذا تسعُلُ في الليلِ تفاصيلُ الأشياء؟ تصحو سُفُني الغارقةُ؛ يُلقِيها البحر على ضِفّةِ روحي، تردِّدُ أسماءَ الموتى كنشيدِ وطني.
وأحاولُ ألا أخجلَ إذ أسمعُها تذكرُ اسمي.
كيف أَعُدُّ الآن نجومي وأصابعُ روحي عالقةٌ بكتابِ التاريخِ كمرساة؟
لا طوقَ نجاة، لا قاربَ، وبلادي يسرقُها المدُّ،
وتسرقُها مثل سريري أحلامُ اليَقَظةِ.
لماذا تسعُلُ في الليلِ تفاصيلُ الأشياء؟
يشتمُني مطرُ الشّكِّ المجنونِ المتسلِّق شباكَ الجيرانِ، وأشْتمه.
والساعةُ واقفةٌ،
وأنا متهمٌ بحراثةِ ماءِ الليلِ،
وخلفي ينسكبُ دواءَ السعال.

7

Why do the details of things cough at night?
My drowning ship awakes; the sea hurls it on the shores of
my soul, the names of the dead repeat like a national anthem.
I try not to be embarrassed if I hear them mention my name.
How do I now count my stars with the fingers of my
soul stuck in the book of history like an anchor?
No life jacket, no boat, and my country stolen by high tide,
like my bed stolen by waking dreams. Why do the details
of things cough at night? The demented rain of doubt
climbing the neighbors' window curses at me, and I curse
back — the clock is still, and I am accused of ploughing the
night's water, while behind me the cough syrup spills.

قططٌ ميّتةٌ تواصلُ المُواءَ

خلفَ سورِ المدرسةِ الابتدائيةِ، بينما يصْطفُّ التلاميذُ لتحيّةِ العَلَمِ، سلخَ الأطفالُ الأصغرُ سنّاً جلودَ القططِ حيّةً، علّقوا الفِراءَ على عِصيٍّ طويلةٍ، طافوا حولَ المدرسةِ يصرخونَ بمُواءٍ مُتَّصلٍ. الآباءُ والأمهاتُ الذين أيقنوا أنّ أبناءَهم صاروا قِططاً، رشّوا شوارعَ الحيِّ بالملحِ ليبدّدوا رائحةَ الغيابِ، غسلوا مراراً ملابسَ الأولادِ المُعدَّةَ لعيدٍ لنْ يأتي.
ضريرٌ كانَ يستمعُ عبرَ مذياعِه لمباراةٍ مُعادةٍ، قالَ لمهرولينَ فضوليينَ: لا تُسرعوا، فالمباراةُ انتهتْ بهزيمةِ الفريقينِ؛ لكنّهم لمْ يَلتقطوا النكتةَ، سرقوا مذياعَهُ، وتركوه يَسبُّ الحكّامَ. في تلكَ الأيامِ لمْ نكترثْ لشكوى الجدرانِ من كثرةِ الدماءِ التي عليها، مَنْ يهتمُّ لجدرانٍ تشكو؟! ذاتَ صباحٍ لم نجدْ البيوتَ، فقطْ أكوامٌ من كلماتٍ حمراءَ تُركتْ مثلَ ملابسَ متّسخةٍ على الأرصفةِ، وأيضاً لَمْ يَعبأْ بها أحدٌ؛ لكنّ الأزواجَ أكملُوا– وبلا جدرانٍ– حياتَهم العاديّةَ؛ بلْ وأنجبوا أطفالاً آخرينَ سلخوا مزيداً من القططِ داخلَ المدرسةِ.
طبيبُ القلبِ الذي يتابعُني لمْ يعدْ يوصي بشيءٍ غيرِ الكَفِّ عن كتابةِ يوميّاتِ قريةٍ ميتةٍ.

DEAD CATS CONTINUE TO MEOW

Behind the walls of the grade school, while the students line
up to salute the flag, the younger kids flay cats alive, they
hang the furs on tall sticks, they circle around the school
with a continuous meow. The parents, who concluded that
their kids became cats, sprinkled salt on the neighborhood
streets to remove the stench of absence, and washed again
and again the children's clothes for a holiday that won't come.
A blind man listening to a match replay on his radio said to
curious runners-by: don't hurry, the match ends with
the defeat of both teams, but they didn't get the joke.
They stole his radio and left him cursing the politicians.
In those days, we didn't pay attention to the complaints
of walls — so much blood was on them, who cares about
walls that complain? One morning, we didn't find homes,
just heaps of red words piled like dirty clothes on sidewalks,
no one cared about them either; couples, though, continued —
and without walls — their usual business, not only that, but
they made more kids who flayed more cats inside the school.
The heart doctor treating me now recommends only one thing:
stop writing the diaries of a dead village.

على من نقرأُ الوقتَ؟

لم تتركْ الحربُ لي غير الذينَ ماتوا أسميهُم الأصدقاءَ. أباركُ ليلاً وانذرُ شمعاً كي يعبرونيَ، في حلمٍ كمبضعٍ أو سعالٍ، لم تتركْ ليَ القلبَ نافذةً أعلقُها على حائطِ الذكرياتِ، ولا شارعاً كلما لوّحَ الوجدُ منديلَهُ هجّتْ طيورٌ وأنّت أغانٍ، فهي لم تنسَ بعدُ طعمَ الرصاصِ النحاسيِّ، ورائحةَ الفراقِ العميقةَ في القلبِ. لمْ تنسَ أن يداً تنثرُ الحبَّ كبائعٍ للجرائدِ على عتباتِ الصباحِ صارتْ تلمُّ اشلاءَهُم كلَ ليلةٍ تحتَ الوسائدِ، وتراصفَهُم في مكتباتِ البيوتِ جوارَ الأماني القديمةِ والقبلِ اليابسةِ. على من إذن نقرأُ الفاتحةَ! والذي ماتَ ماتَ، وفي كفِّهِ سلةُ الخضرواتِ ورائحةُ الفاكهةِ، ماتَ وفي جيبِهِ تذكرةُ الباصِ ووصفةُ البيتزا الجديدةِ! على من إذن نقرأُ الوقتَ، فلم يبقَ على رصيفِ الشوقِ لم يركبْ الحافلةَ سواي وركضُ الصباحِ؛ حيث لم تترك لنا الحربُ غير المسافةِ بين بائعِ الوردِ والمقبرة.

TO WHOM SHOULD WE RECITE THE TIME?

The war left me only those who died to call friends. I bless night and light a votive candle so they pass through me in a dream, like a scalpel or a cough, it left me no heart as a window to hang on the wall of memories, no street for when passion waves its kerchief and birds flee and songs groan because it didn't forget the coppery taste of bullets and the deep scent of parting in the heart. It didn't forget that a hand scattering love like a news vendor on morning doorsteps now collects their remains every night under the pillows, it arranges them in family libraries next to old wishes and stale kisses. To whom then should we recite The Opening? Whoever died died, in their palm a basket of vegetables and the scent of fruit, and in their pocket a bus ticket and a new recipe for pizza! To whom then should we recite the Time, for no one is left on the sidewalk of longing who didn't get on the bus but me and the morning rush, where war left us nothing but the distance between the florist and the cemetery.

في الحَربِ التي لا تنتهي

ضَعُوا قلوبَكمْ تَحتَ الأَسرَّةِ أحذيةً مُرهقةً مُهملةً، فلا يَمُرّ غبارُ الحروبِ عليها، ولا تعرفون.
ضَعُوا قلوبَكم على الرفِّ ساعةً قديمةً معطلةً، فلا رعشةُ القصف تعبرُكم ولا تحزنون.
في الحربِ يتّسعُ القلبُ، يصيرُ قارباً للصغارِ، ساعةً للصفاءِ،
سماءً للكتابةِ.
في الحربِ يختنقُ القلبُ، تَهجُّ الكلماتُ، تذوبُ على حافتِه العصافيرُ ندىً أحمرَ، يرفرفُ على ساريةٍ شاهقةٍ، شاهقةٍ، يسمونها الوطن.
في الحربِ تتركُ قلبكَ جانباً وتنقذُ صُرَّةَ الأوراقِ: صورتكَ القديمةَ عند بابِ المدرسةِ، مِلكيّةَ بيتكَ المهدومِ، شهادةَ ميلادِ لأبنكَ، قلبُكَ لا يهمُّ الآن. ستنتظرُ الحبيبةُ انتهاءَ الحربِ كي تسألَ: هلْ كنتَ تذكرُني؟
في الحربِ لا أحدَ يصدّقُ قلبكَ المحزونَ. يصعدُ المسعفونَ على ساعدَيكَ لِيُسندوا سقفَ البكاءِ، الطائراتُ تحُطُ حولَكَ ظِلَّها، وتطيرُ روحُكَ مثلَ سربٍ من زجاجٍ. الوقتُ أنتَ ولا يدلُّ شظيةً على الروحِ غيرُكَ، ربّما تشتاقُ أنْ ترمي على الأولادِ قلبكَ طابةً، ربّما تشتاقُ أن تفتحَ الشباكَ دونَ رصاصةِ امرأةٍ طائشةٍ، لا بأسَ هي حربٌ واحدةٌ أخرى وتمضي.
في الحربِ ينتحرُ الوقتُ،
يمرُّ اليومُ حينَ تُتاحُ دورةُ المياهِ لكَ، والساعةُ فسحةٌ ما بينَ بنايةِ عانقَتْها القذيفةُ، وأخرَى تفتحُ صدرَها للشهيقِ الأخيرِ في شارعٍ سيغادرُ التاريخَ حالاً، والدقيقةُ؟! لا دقائقَ في الحربِ، حيثُ يُقاسُ الوقتُ بالشهداءِ: مئةً، وألفاً.

IN THE ENDLESS WAR

Put your hearts under the beds — exhausted neglected shoes
not to be covered by the dust of war:
"and you shall not know."
Put your hearts away on the shelf like an old and broken clock,
so the raid won't shake them:
"and you shall not be sad."
In war the heart expands, becoming a boat for the children,
an hour of clarity, and a sky for writing.
In war the heart chokes, words flee, and along its edge birds
melt into red dew. Fluttering on a towering staff, a gasp called
the homeland. In war you leave your heart aside and you
salvage a bundle of paper: your old picture at the school gate,
the deed of your demolished home, your son's birth certificate.
Your heart doesn't matter now. The beloved will await war's
end to ask: did you remember me?
In war no one believes your grief-stricken heart.
The rescuers scale your arms to hold up the roof of cries,
the planes land their shadows around you, and your soul
flies out like a flock of glass.
You are time and no one but you guides shrapnel to the soul.
Maybe you'll miss throwing your heart at your children
like a ball. Maybe you'll miss opening the window
without the bullet of a stray woman. It's alright, it's war,
another one and it will pass.
In war, time kills itself.

في الحربِ نجلسُ، حيثُ لا سيقانَ تحمِلُنا لنركضَ.

في الحربِ تتبعُكَ القذيفةُ مثلَ كلبٍ وفيٍّ، وجارٍ مملٍّ يبادلُكَ التحيّةَ والنكتةَ السيئةَ، تحفرُ في الذكرياتِ وشماً على شكلِ بيتٍ، كانَ بيتاً جميلاً قبلَ وصولِ القذيفةِ.

في الحربِ يخجلُ الأبناءُ من نزوَاتِهم، يكبرونَ أمامَنا كأنّا نلتقي بجيرانٍ قُدامى؛ كيف حالُك يا بُنيَّ؟ ما زلتُ أركضُ يا أبي، ما زلتُ أركضُ، واحداً في سباقِ الجنونِ.

في الحربِ أنتَ أدخلْتَنِي التجربةَ، أنتَ من جرَّ غِيلانَ الخُرافةِ نحوَ بابي، أنتَ من نسيَ الشواءِ على الجمرِ عمداً، وأصرخُ: إنّه قلبي، ولمْ تسمعْ، ولمْ تغفِرْ، ولمْ تتركْ من الحُبِّ شيئاً فيه؛ من الكرهِ شيئاً كي أُتِمَّ القصيدةَ.

The day goes by when it's your turn for the bathroom.
The hour is that space between a building embraced
by a missile and another one opening its chest for
the last person gasping on a street about to exit history
instantaneously, as for the minute, no minutes in war,
time is better measured by martyrs: a hundred and a thousand.
In war we sit, no legs to carry us and run.
In war a missile follows you like a loyal dog and a boring
neighbor exchanging greetings and bad jokes.
You etch a tattoo shaped like home into memory.
It was a beautiful home before the arrival of the missile.
In war the children are embarrassed by their tantrums,
they grow before us as if we're meeting old neighbors.
How are you, son? I'm still running father, I'm still running,
alone in the madness race.
In war you brought me into the experience. You're the one who
dragged the mythical ghouls to my door. You're the one who
planned to forget the meat on the grill's burning embers, and I'm
screaming: it's my heart. You did not hear and you did not
forgive. Of love, you left nothing; of hate, you left nothing
for me to finish the poem.
Then you, like a pale cloud of smoke, deceived me into safety.

في الحربِ أنتَ خدعْتَني بالنجاةِ شاحباً كسحابةِ من دخانٍ.
في الحربِ تغبطُكَ الحياةُ على الحياةِ، بيوتُ الغرغرينا، نوافذُ الهستيريا، وإكزيما الشوارع، كلٌّ ما في المشهدِ المذعورِ يغبِطُ أنّكَ تُبصرُ كلَّ هذا، وليس يمكنُكَ البكاءُ.
في الحربِ لست من لحمٍ ودمٍ، أنتَ آخَرُ في نفسِ الثيابِ، مُدمّاةً ومُتسخاتٍ وكاذبةً، وتشهدُ أنَّكَ لمْ تمُتْ بعْد.

In war life envies you for life. Gangrene homes, windows of
hysteria, and the eczema of streets, everything in the horrifying
scene resents that you could see it all and not cry.
In war you're not made of flesh and bones, you're someone
else in the same clothes bloodied, dirty, and lying —
testifying that you're not dead yet.

قالت القصيدةُ كلمتَها

قالت القصيدةُ كلمتَها، ومَضتْ،
لم يعدْ حفلٌ ولا طقسُ ولادة، لم يعد ناي يدلُّ الذاهبينَ إلى صلاةِ الوجد، لم يعدْ غيمٌ يبادلُني المديحَ ولا شجرٌ ينادي بأسمائيَ الحُسنى أو يمدُّ لي ظلّي، أصلّي لنافذةٍ أصلُها قلبي وفرعُها في الحنين.
قالت القصيدةُ كلمتَها، ومضت، وأما اللغةُ فكانت لمساكينَ يعملونَ في حديقة، وكان وراءَهم وردٌ وسروٌ ونبيذ يؤمُّ سنابلَ اغنيات، حينَ تَركوا كلّ هذا واتّبعوا أثرَ القصيدةِ حتى مطلعِ الشمس، وأمّا المعنى فكان سراباً أتبعُه، ويتبعُني. كان بياضاً يطفو على ماءٍ آسن، فقلتُ له: كنْ، فلم يكن، وقلتُ له: لا تكن، فكان بياضاً يطفو على ماءٍ آسن، وكنتُ على حافةِ الماء أشاهدُ وجهي وأنكرُه، أشاهدُ وجهي وأنكرُه، وخلفي ألفُ ديكٍ يصيح.
قالت القصيدةُ كلمتَها ومضتْ،
لم يعدْ قلمٌ لأفتح في مدى الفقهاءِ عكا، ولا سيف لأقطعَ يداً من سارقي أحلامي، ماذا أقولُ الآن للشباكِ حينَ ينقُرُني الحمام! ماذا أقولُ للشرطي وهو يُعدُّ لي كرسي اعترافي؟ لصيدِ غزالةٍ ماذا أقولُ، وللمدى الجالسِ القرفصاءَ في بياضِ الصفحةِ الأولى؟ ماذا تقولُ طاولةٌ وحدها لحصارِ الكراسي؟ وماذا تقول الحبيبةُ الخرساء حين يعود حبيبُها من الصمتِ الطويل؟ ماذا يقول سفرٌ لعاشقَين يؤمهم حب المكان؟ ومن سيفسرُ سورةَ الرملِ وهي بلَّلَها بكاءُ الأنبياء؟
منْ كان يعرفُ أنّ لي ساقاً، والريحُ طبلُ خيولِها، لأخوضَ بحراً لا ضفافَ له، وأرجعُ للخليفةِ كلّ يومٍ وفي كفّي مدينة؟ أو أن لي ليلاً يفتشُ عن

THE POEM SAID ITS PIECE

The poem said its piece, and moved on, no longer ceremony
nor rite of birth, no longer flute to guide those going to the
prayer of ecstasy, no longer clouds to return my praise, and
no longer trees to invoke my divine names or lengthen my
shadow, I pray to a window rooted in my heart that branches
into longing. The poem said its piece and moved on, as for
the language it was destined for miserable people working
in a garden, behind them roses, cypress, and wine leading in
prayer grain stalks of song, when they left all this behind to
follow the trace of the poem until the rising of the sun,
as for the meaning it was a mirage, I follow it and it follows
me. It was white floating on stagnant water, so I said to it:
be, and it didn't, and I said: do not be, then it was white
floating on stagnant water, and I was at the water's edge
looking at my face and disowning it, I look at my face and
disown it, while behind me a thousand roosters crow.
The poem said its piece, and moved on, no longer a pen for
me to open a breach like Akka in the theologians' reach, and
no longer a sword to sever the hand of the thief of my dreams,
what should I say now to the window when I'm pecked by
doves! What should I to say to the policeman as he readies
the chair for my confession? What should I say — in a hunt
for the gazelle, to the expanse squatting on the whiteness of
the first page . . . ?
All by itself, what does a table say to the siege of chairs?

مراياها حثيثاً، ويَرمي في كلِّ نافذةٍ نهاراً من جنونٍ وهُتاف؟؟ من كان يعرفُ أنّ لي شفة الغناء، ولثغة الأطفال، أو أن لي رنة الأجراس حين يرفعُ شعرَكِ ثم يتركُه الهواءُ؟
قالت القصيدةُ كلمتَها، ومضتْ،
الآنَ أجلسُ فاتراً أعد على أصابعها جراحي، وكم تبقّى من جنودي، أسيري وحده ندمي، ونديمي، وخبزُ عشائي الأخير.

What does a mute lover say to her mate when he's back from
long silence? What does travel say to lovers led in prayer by
the attachment to place? Who will interpret the Sura of Sand,
now wet from the tears of the Prophets? Who knew I had
a leg, and wind the drum of its horses, to wade into
a shoreless sea, coming back daily to the Caliph
with a city in the palm of my hand? Or that I have a night
looking intently for its mirror as it casts a day of madness
and clamor into every window? Who knew that I had the lip
for singing, the lisp of children, or the ring of bells when air
lifts and drops your hair.
The poem said its piece, and moved on, now I sit listless
counting my wounds on its fingers, how many of my soldiers
remain, regret my only captive, my faithful companion,
and the bread of my last supper.

تماثيلَ من لحمٍ ودمٍ

غادروا، لمْ يطفئوا خلفَهمْ قمرَ الحنينِ، لم يُغلقوا باباً يُطلُّ على ندى خطواتِهم، لم يشربوا ماءً ليعرفوا كيفَ الرجوعُ إلى المياه، إلى مساءٍ يسندُ وجهَهُ بيدِ الغيابِ، واضحينَ في الحكايةِ غادروا، غائمينَ في الدموع. تماثيلَ من لحمٍ ودمٍ، عابسين، مبتسمين . . . كيفَما شئنا نراهم. مزّقوا أحلامَهم، وارتدوا أحلامَنا، غادروا، تاركين حَبّاً وافراً لفخاخِ الذكرياتِ، لطيورِ رغبتِنا اللّحوحةِ في العتابِ، لَم ينظروا خلفهم، غادروا وقتاً، واستظلّوا بآخرَ، حيث لا أعينَ تضحكُ ثَمَّ، ولا بكاء.

١٩ نوفمبر/ تشرين الثاني ٢٠٢٣

STATUES OF FLESH AND BLOOD

They left without turning the moon of longing off behind them,
without shutting the door overlooking the dew of the steps
they'd taken, they don't drink water to know how to return
to water, they head towards an evening leaning its face against
the hand of absence, lucid about the business of leaving,
and overcome by tears. They are statues of flesh and blood,
frowning, smiling . . . any which way we want to see them.
They tore their dreams down, put ours on, and left,
leaving heaps of seed on the traps of memory, for the birds of
our nagging wish to blame, not looking back, they left one
time to take shelter in another, where no eyes smile or cry.

November 19, 2023

بدون عنوان

ومرَّ يومٌ، ودباباتٌ، والسماءُ حفلٌ لأطفالٍ على شكلِ طائراتٍ ورقيةٍ، وسالتْ دماءٌ خلفَ سيارةٍ لاهثة.
ومرَّ يومٌ، وطائراتٌ، وخيمةُ النازحينَ كانت تراهنُ الوقتَ: إنّ الشتاءَ تأخرَ.
ومرَّ يومٌ، وقناصونَ، والسوقُ نفسه لم يجد مِلحاً، فَقلت: لا بأسَ، فحزنُ البائعينَ كان وفيراً.
ومرَّ يومٌ، ومدافعٌ، غيرَ أنّ جنازةَ جاري بطيئةٌ، فمَن يتعجّل في مِثلِ وقتٍ كهذا!
ومرَّ يومٌ، ونشراتُ أخبار، وجاءَ المساءُ، وكانَ سعيداً قليلاً، حيثُ وَجَدَنا، ولمْ يتغيّب مِنّا أَحَد سِوى البيت.

٣٠ ديسمبر/ كانون الأول ٢٠٢٣

UNTITLED

And a day goes by, and tanks, and the sky a festival of kids
flying kites, and blood flowed behind a panting car.
And a day goes by, and the planes, and the tent of
the displaced makes a bet with time: winter is late.
And a day goes by, and the snipers, and the market
itself has no salt: so I said: No worries,
the merchants have plenty of sadness.
And a day goes by, and artillery, but my neighbor's
funeral passes along slowly, why rush at a time like this!
And a day goes by, and the newscasts,
and when evening came,
it was a bit joyous to find us all there
and none missing, except the house.

December 30, 2023

خارِج مِن البيتِ

لا عليكَ، إنْ لمْ تَجِد للبيتِ حينَ خَرجتَ أذرُعاً للعِناقِ،
إنْ لمْ ترَ عَينيهِ كَي تَدلَّهُما أينَ خَبّأتَ صُرَّةَ الأَسى،
وإنْ لمْ يَكُن لَهُ كَتِفٌ لِتهمسَ عندهُ بالمحبةِ،
وتوصيه على بقيةِ الثيابِ، على خزانةِ الصحونِ، وما تيسَّرَ مِنْ
دَواءِ السعالِ،
لا تَكن ضَجِراً إنْ تعلّقتْ بساقَيك الذِكْرَيات مِثل طفلةٍ يتيمةٍ، ولمْ تَشأ
البَقاء، خُذْها معك، مثل كيس الطحين وجرّة الغاز وقَطرة العَينِ، ستجِد
لها مكاناً حيثُ تكون.
لا تقلْ لها بحكمتِكَ الباليةِ: إبقِ، لتُؤنِسي البَيتَ ولا تدعِيه وحدَهُ
يعبرُ التجربةَ،
لا عليكَ، فالبيتُ طِفلُكَ الذي دلَّلْتَهُ، صارَ شاباً سيَحْتَمِلُ الوحدةَ
والرصاص، طفلُكَ الذي ربّيْتَه صارَ شاباً سيَحْتَمِلُ الحربَ ويتذوّقُ للمرةِ
الأولى لكماتِ الدبابات،
لا عليكَ، ستراهُ مُتعَباً حينَ تعودُ إليهِ، نعم، جريحاً، ربما،
لكنّهُ واثقاً من وقوفِه، يهذِهدُ روحَهُ المفتَّتَة، يَلُمُّ على صدرِهِ
نوافذَهُ الممزقة،
وأنتَ كأبٍ يحارُ كيفَ يضمِّد جراحَ البيتِ.

١ مارس/ آذار ٢٠٢٤

LEAVING THE HOUSE

It's not on you, that when you left you realized House had no
arms to embrace, that you didn't see its eyes to guide them to
where you hid the bundle of sorrow, and that it didn't have a
shoulder upon which to whisper love, ask to attend to the rest
of the clothes, the china cabinet, and what's left of the cough
medicine, don't be uneasy if memories cling to your legs like
an orphaned girl, and if they don't want to stay, take them
with you, like the bag of flour and the canister of gas and
the eye drops, you'll find a place for them wherever you are.
Don't tell them with your worn-out wisdom, stay to keep
House company, don't let it go through this alone.
It's not on you — House, your child that you coddled,
is now a young man who will endure loneliness and bullets.
The kid you raised is a man who will endure war, and taste
the jabs of tanks for the first time, it's not on you, you'll see
it fatigued when you come back to it, yes, wounded maybe,
but still sure in its standing, cradling its shattered spirit,
drawing the shredded windows to its chest, and you,
like a Father, puzzled as to how to dress House's wounds.

March 1, 2024

آخر الجنود

ها أنتَ تُلقي مَوعِظةً بالصمتِ على كومةِ الميتينَ، وتَمضي، تَماماً كأنّكَ تسألُ بائعَ الخُضرواتِ عن شيءٍ، وتَمضي.
وهكذا يُواصلُ السبتُ ركضَهُ متعباً حتى الخميسِ،
يحاولُ دونَ جدوى أن يُصدِّق نَشرةَ الأخبارِ،
كَبيتِهِ المَهْدومِ يَودُّ لو يفرُّ مِن ثيابِه،
يَدورُ في مَكانِه من ظهيرةٍ لمساءٍ مِثلَ عَقْرَبِ السّاعاتِ،
يَوَدُّ لَو تَوقَّفَ كلّ شيءٍ؛
إلى الغدِ لا تأخُذِيني أيتها الحربُ،
ماذا سأصْنَعُ في صبيحةِ غدٍ يَجِيءُ بِلا أصدقاءَ؟
غيرَ أنّهُ لا يَجِدُ شَيئاً يَدُلُّ على انتهاءِ الحربِ غيرَ احتمالٍ باهتٍ: أَنْ تَصْدأَ الدبابةُ الأخيرةُ،
أو يَموتَ آخرُ الجنودِ.

٧ مارس/ آذار ٢٠٢٤

THE LAST OF THE SOLDIERS

There you are, giving a silent sermon over a heap
of the dead and move on, just like when you ask the grocer
for something, and move on. And so goes Saturday running
tired till Thursday, it tries in vain to believe the news,
like his destroyed home, wanting to flee from its clothes
it runs around in circles from afternoon to evening like
the hands of a clock, wishing everything would stop, don't
take me to the next day, O war, what am I supposed to do
the morning of another day that shows up without friends?
Yet it finds nothing to signal the end of war except
the slight chance: for the last tank to rust,
or the last of the soldiers to die.

March 7, 2024

غضب

لم تكنْ أنتَ مَنْ شاهَدوُه على شاشةِ التلفاز،
لم تكن أنتَ وهم يصوِّرونَكَ خارجاً مفتَّتاً مِن الركامِ،
فمَن ذا الذي كانَ يصفِّقُ للموتِ ويهتفُ لهُ؟
هكذا إذن تصنَعُكَ الحربُ، تنزعُ عنكَ جلدَكَ وتُعطي لَكَ خيمةً،
ومثل ورقة مجعدة تَرمي إلى مَكبّ النفاياتِ بيتَك،
تقطفُ قلبَك الوردي، وتغرُسُ حجرَ البارود،
لا حقولاً من القمحِ تلمعُ في عينيك بعد الآن، لا تِلالاً من الزيتونِ تحلمُ
بالقطافِ، لا روضةَ الأطفالِ تلهو على كَتِفَيك، لا عشبَ التذكرِ يُجالِسُك
في غروبِ البيت.
لا شيءَ هنا أو هناك سوى غضبٍ لا يَنتهي،
يفيضُ إلى نهايةِ الزمانِ والمسافةِ،
لم تكن أنتَ، لم يكن جدولُ ماءٍ، كان ذئباً يزمجرُ تحتَ الركام،
يودُّ لو يأكل بأسنانِه لحمَ هذه الدباباتِ.

١٣ مارس/ آذار ٢٠٢٤

RAGE

It wasn't you they saw on the television screen, it wasn't you
as they filmed you coming out crumbled from the rubble,
who then was applauding and clamoring for death?
This is what war makes you: it takes your skin off and gives
you a tent, and like a crumpled piece of paper, it throws
your home out with the trash—it plucks your pink heart
and plants gunpowder stones, no wheat fields gleam in
your eyes from now on, no hills of olive groves dream
to be picked, no bunch of kids play on your shoulders,
no grass of remembrance sits with you in the sunset
of the house, nothing here or there except limitless
rage, boiling over to the end of time and distance,
it was not you; it was not a stream of water, it was
a wolf snarling underneath the rubble, wanting
to rip the flesh of these tanks with its teeth.

March 13, 2024

جوع

ربما قطٌّ يمرُّ آخرَ الليلِ،
ربما الأكاسيا تموءُ تحتَ الركامِ،
وليسَ من البردِ ترتعشُ البيوتُ،
بينما الجوعُ يعوي، يعوي في الشمال.
يمرُّ يومٌ ويومٌ وليلةٌ ولا يستيقظُ ابنُ الجيرانِ،
يمرُّ يومٌ ويومٌ وليلةٌ، والغبارُ يواصلُ نومَتَهُ على حِبال الغسيلِ،
لكن إلى أين يا تُرى اصْطَحَبَتْ جيراني القذيفةُ؟
وأنا أكذبُ حين أقولُ: يا أصدقائي لا بأس،
كلُّ موتٍ يُحْتَمَل، كلُّ شيءٍ يُحْتَمَل، كلُّ غِيابٍ يَمُرُّ،
سِوى جُوعُ أصدقائي في الشمال.

١٨ مارس/ آذار ٢٠٢٤

HUNGER

Maybe a tomcat passes by late at night,
maybe an acacia meows under the rubble,
and it isn't from cold the houses shiver,
while hunger howls, it howls in the North.
A day passes, and a day and a night, and
the neighbors' son doesn't wake up,
a day passes, and a day and a night, and
dust continues sleeping on the clotheslines.
But where did the shell take my neighbors?
And I'd be lying when I say: friends, it's alright.
Every death is bearable, every
thing is bearable, every absence passes,
except the hunger of my friends in the North.

March 18, 2024

فتات الكراسي

شهراً كاملاً أراوغُ الركام.
يحومُ حولي، ولا أرى سوى البيت مثلما كان قبل الحطام.
أمامي الركام، وعيناي تفتحُ الأبواب، تصهل الكمنجات في عروقي،
تجولان في الممراتِ لامعةً معطرةً، فأنتشي، ترتب السريرَ كأنَّ عليه
الغبارَ، فأسعلُ، تغلق الشبابيك خشية المطر، أنحني للريح، تدور كأنها
تبحث عن جواربي التائهة، فلا أجدني.
شهر كامل من الجدال،
ذاكرة عنيدة ومشهد صاخب من الفتات،
بيت جميل وعائلة صامتة،
حزن طويل.. طويل حتى رجوع الكهرباء.
ألم يكن شهراً كافياً ليحتمل الوقوف على ساقيه قلبي؟
لعيني أن تبصرا حرقة الخراب؟ أما آن لذاكرتي إحتمال الدواء لتصحو؟
وليدي وهي تصعد درج الورد فلا يبللها دم الأسى؟
شهراً، ومن ينسى حنان الستائر، رقة الرخام، شرفة الأغاني؟
شهرا، وللأولاد كي ينضج العشاء، ها قد طاوعتك يداك لتشعل لهم
فتات الكراسي!

٣٢ مارس/ آذار ٢٠٢٤

PIECES OF CHAIRS

A full month of me circumventing the rubble.
It runs around me, and all I see is home before the wreckage.
Rubble in front of me, and my eyes open the doors, violins
neigh in my veins, my eyes roam along the shiny, fragrant
hallways, and I'm elated, wreckage makes the bed,
it's dusty and I cough, it shuts the windows, afraid of rain,
and I bend in the wind, it runs around like it's looking
for my vagrant socks, and I can't find myself.
A full month of back and forth,
a stubborn memory and a loud scene of bits and pieces,
a beautiful home and a silent family, a long sadness . . .
as long as it takes for the power to come back.
Wasn't a month enough for my heart to stand on its own
two feet? For my eyes to see the grief of destruction? Isn't it
time for my memory to stomach the medicine and wake up?
Or for my hands, as they climb the stairs of roses, not to be
stained by the blood of sorrow?
A month on, who can forget the tenderness of the curtains,
the softness of marble, the balcony of song?
A month on, look, you got your hands to burn pieces
of chairs to cook dinner for the kids!

March 23, 2024

ساحةٌ من رماد

الآنَ والأخبارُ غاضبةٌ، وقلبي شاحبٌ ودمي غبار،
الآنَ، لا بيتَ يدِلُّ شارِعَنا على سكانِه، لا شارعَ يدِلُّ مدينةً بأكملِها على النسيان، كيف محى الطريقُ خطى المساءِ مَشَت عليه؟ وكيف تنكّرَ الدوري فجأةً لشرفتِنا الصغيرة؟
لا سيارةَ المشفى أوصلت دَمَنا، ولا نحن جَوْعى، وأكمَلنا قُبَيلَ النومِ وجبةَ الحطامِ.
القلبُ ساحةٌ من رماد، يتوافدُه الحفّارونَ صباحَ مساءَ، ينبُشون قبورَ أصحابي القدامى، ويسرِقونَ لي خشبَ الذكرياتِ.
الآنَ والأخبارُ صاخبةٌ، ويدي مدى، ودمي نهار.
الآنَ، والتاريخُ عادتُنا، سنفتَح بابَ قلعتِنا لطاعونِ التتار،
والتاريخُ لعبتُنا، هي خيمةٌ أولى فقط وتكاثرَتْ، وكأنّها تعويذةُ الشعبِ الذي أحبَّ هجرتَه كي لا يموت، كي يصِلَ المدينةَ العنقاء في أحلامه، ويقيمَ هناك بيتاً من حُطامِ سفينةِ نوح. والغارُ خيمتُنا، وسُراقة يمتطي دبّابة، يفتش عن سوارِ النازحين.

PLAZA OF ASH

Now that the news is furious, my heart is pale, and my
blood is dust, now, no home is there to guide our street to its
residents, no street is there to guide an entire city to oblivion,
how did the road erase the footsteps of evening that walked it?
And how did the sparrow suddenly ignore our small balcony?
No ambulance delivers our blood, nor do we go hungry after
we finish the meal of wreckage before bedtime.
The heart is a plaza of ash with diggers coming and going
all day, exhuming the graves of my old friends, and stealing
the wood of my memory. Now that the news is raucous,
my hand is limit, and my blood day. And now,
with history our ritual, we'll open the gate of our citadel
to the Tatars' plague, and with history our game, one tent
and it multiplies, as if it was an incantation for a people who love
their migration in order to survive, to reach the City
of the Phoenix in their dreams, and there build a home
from the wreckage of Noah's Ark. And the cave is our tent,
and Suraqa rides a tank, looking for the bracelet of the
displaced. Nothing tempts us more than the thrill of escaping
the mundane, that we die, we die, and we don't die
nothing lures us more than those caring for our death
like it was an apple just half ours
with the other belonging to the wind.

لا شيء يغوينا إلا مهابةُ الإفلاتِ من إطارِ المشهدِ العادي، هو أن نموتَ وأن نموتَ وأن نموتَ ولا نموت، لا شيء يغوينا سوى اكتراثُ الآخرينَ بموتِنا وكأنّه تفاحةٌ، نِصفُها ليست لنا، ونِصفُها للريح.
يا غزة الملعونة المحبوبة المجنونة المقهورة المنبوذة المفتونة المنسيَّة المذكورة ألف مرة في كتاب الحربِ، لا أنتِ ربّةُ الموتى ولا كتابك اسمه حزن البلاد.

١٢ أبريل/ نيسان ٢٠٢٤

O Gaza, accursed, beloved, deranged, oppressed, outcast,
enchanted, forgotten, mentioned a thousand times
in the Book of War, you're not the Goddess of the Dead,
nor is your book called Sorrow of the Country.

April 12, 2024

TRANSLATORS' AFTERWORD

Our first encounter with the poetry of Nasser Rabah was through Mosab Abu Toha, with whom Ammiel Alcalay has been in conversation since 2018. A constant in their exchange has been the need to translate more work from Gaza. Having initiated the collective translation project of Syrian poet and former political prisoner Faraj Bayrakdar with the late scholar and translator Shareah Taleghani, Ammiel thought such an approach the best way to proceed. To that end, he brought together Emna Zghal and Khaled al-Hilli, two friends with very different backgrounds, to work in collaboration. Emna is a visual artist and professional interpreter for whom poetry in a number of languages has always been a primary source, while Khaled is a professor of Arabic whose knowledge, love of language, and life experience has immersed him in Arabic as written and spoken across a varied geographic and generic range.

When Mosab provided us with a selection from a number of Gazan poets whose work he felt should be made available in translation, he emphasized Nassar Rabah as essential among them. Emna immediately gravitated to what she's described as Nasser's irreverent, free voice, its elevated language infused with a profoundly erudite and nuanced use of classical Arabic sources, and the way in which some of these sources are, counter-intuitively, treated as common knowledge. This presents formidable challenges on many different levels for translation into American English in coherent cultural terms. Our first efforts resulted in the publication of two longer poems, "In the Endless War," and "Background Music for Life" (involving Addison Bale and Elsa Saade as collaborators), in a special issue of the *Michigan Review* in 2021, submitted just months before the May 2021 Israeli assault on Gaza. The poems resonated widely, and Emna began communicating directly with Nasser as we prepared to work on a longer selection for a possible book. Given that this would be Nasser Rabah's first collection in translation, our aim was to provide as broad an entry as possible to this major poet. And given that his books published in Arabic are not easy to find, we hoped to present this work in a bilingual edition, for readers in Arabic who are not yet familiar with it.

As our work began in earnest, we sometimes spent hours on several lines as we slowly learned how to read Nasser's poetry. At a certain point, as the lines we struggled over began to fit into the bigger picture, we realized that we were also thinking about our translations in ways that might help to guide readers and lead them into and around Nasser's world. In that sense, whether we were translating single poems, or serial poems, we were looking at his work as a whole and trying to pinpoint those poems that would give a coherent picture of his poetry as part of a life's work. And in the end, our selection would aim to reproduce this layered interpretive process, sequencing the work in such a way that, finally, the poems themselves teach us how to read them.

Collective translation is an extraordinary process of give and take, and we attempted what is most difficult: to avoid over-translating while maintaining ambiguity and even non-understanding. There are times when this can make for unusual syntax or phrases in the translation, but never more unusual than in the original. Given the paradoxical situation of bringing this work into the very language—American English—that plays a role in enabling so many of the distortions in how Palestine is depicted on the world stage, we have attuned ourselves to bending English toward the syntax, rhythm, and idiosyncrasies of Arabic. But in order not to exoticize the original, we sought every available nook and cranny where freedom remains in a language that too often feels as if much of its own native energy has been sapped by the surround sound of propaganda and conventional writing produced for commercial consumption.

Even with our own familiarity and personal connections to the long history and stark realities of recurrent Israeli attacks on Gaza, after October 7, 2023 it became clear very quickly that what Nasser, and all Gazans, and all Palestinians were now up against was of a completely different order of magnitude. And it also became clear—as we became more familiar with the range of Nasser's poetry and began to see the new poems emerging from his experience under the genocidal assault —that we were in the presence of a singularly powerful and unique poet.

Needless to say, the process of completing this translation was not an ordinary experience, limited to the literary tasks at hand. We worked with a sense of urgency, in touch with Nasser whenever and however possible, and our relationship to him and his family became that of extended kin: we rejoiced and felt relief at the birth of a granddaughter, the retrieval of a canister of cooking gas, the discovery of pavers brought home to build an oven for baking bread, the poetry written by younger daughter Sahar, news of putting up a net for kids to play volleyball in the neighborhood, and actual survival through continual aerial, artillery, drone, quad-copter, infantry, and sniper attacks, not to mention the lack of water, food, electricity, medicine, and almost everything else, including sleep. There was a long and terrifying period of no contact when the family was displaced, then joy at news of their safety, and further dismay at a video clip of the ruins of Nasser's study and library, as he held the first book pulled from the rubble that came to hand, *War and Peace*.

While we seldom burdened him with questions about specific meanings until the very last stages, along the way Nasser often expressed both pity and wonder at our efforts: pity that anyone living in a more-or-less ordered society would trouble themselves with such poetic enigmas and wonder that we actually remained committed to carrying it through. But, as he messaged us at some point: "All this fatigue with my poems will not be in vain. At least I'm getting through the war with my head held high and my heart at peace."

This work has sustained us as well, and as translators, the idea that we might, somehow, be able to contribute to the poet's own sense of himself and the import of his work, especially at such a critical time, is the highest and most meaningful recognition possible.

In a short piece written in late 2023, Nasser had this to say about a topic that, while being part and parcel of his work, has never fully defined it, and the distinction is crucial: "War refines life, it explains anew your very being; war might also make you reconsider your understanding of time and history. Are you really what you claim to be, with attributes of humanity, civilization, culture, beauty, rebellion, and creativity? Or are you someone entirely different from what you've imagined one day?" As we write this, life in Gaza has become apocalyptic in every sense of the word. All human norms are in the process of being shattered: the form, image and idea of the human—of a child, a sibling, a mother, a father, a doctor, a teacher, a journalist, a farmer, a medic, an ambulance driver, an engineer, a municipal worker, a student—all are under unprecedented attack, aided by heretofore never deployed technologies, all of this being shown to us live, around the clock. And despite the powerlessness that the exhibition of such atrocities inculcates, resistance to this shattering cruelty is fierce. Nasser Rabah is one of our most attentive and trustworthy guides to this world, the world that actually exists, whether we are subjected to such assaults or not, whether we make any attempt to resist, or not. His poetry is important in ways we have yet to comprehend, and we are grateful for this opportunity to present some of it in this collection.

Ammiel Alcalay, Emna Zghal, and Khaled al-Hilli

NASSER RABAH is a Palestinian poet and novelist born in Gaza in 1963. He got his BA in Agricultural Science in 1985, before going on to work as Director of the Communication Department in the Agriculture Ministry. He is a member of the Palestinian Writers and Authors Union and has published five collections of poetry, *Running After Dead Gazelles* (2003); *One of Nobody* (2011); *Passersby with Light Clothes* (2014); *Water Thirsty for Water* (2017); *Eulogy for the Robin* (2021), and two novels, *Since approximately an hour* (2018), and *The Enclosure of the Gazelle* (2024). His poems have been translated into English, French, Hebrew, and Spanish. He lives in Gaza.

AMMIEL ALCALAY, poet, novelist, translator, essayist, critic, and scholar, has published over 20 books, including *After Jews and Arabs, Memories of Our Future, Islanders,* and the forthcoming *CONTROLLED DEMOLITION: a work in four books,* and *Follow the Person: Archival Encounters.*

KHALED AL-HILLI teaches Arabic at New York University. His doctoral research in Comparative Literature at the CUNY Graduate Center was on the post 2003 Iraqi novel, and his *Sargon Boulos: "This Great River" Translating the Beats into Arabic*, was published by Lost & Found in 2024.

EMNA ZGHAL is a Brooklyn-based visual artist trained in both Tunisia and the United States. Reviews of her exhibits have appeared in the *New Yorker,* the *New York Times,* and *Artforum*, among other publications. Noted public collections include the Newark Museum, Flint Institute of Art, Yale University Library, the New York Public Library, the Africa Center, NY, and the Schomburg Center for Research in Black Culture, NY.